Hunting
RECORD-BOOK
BUCKS

BY TOBY BRIDGES

CREATIVE
PUBLISHING
international

MINNETONKA, MINNESOTA

www.creativepub.com

TOBY BRIDGES has been hunting whitetails since the early 1960s, with modern rifle, shotgun, muzzleloader and bow. He is recognized as one of the country's leading outdoor writers, with more than 1,200 articles and a dozen books published. Toby is also considered today's leading authority on muzzleloader hunting, and is the author of the award-winning book *Muzzleloading*, also published by Creative Publishing international.

President/CEO: Michael Eleftheriou
Vice President/Publisher: Linda Ball

HUNTING RECORD-BOOK BUCKS
By Toby Bridges

Executive Editor, Outdoor Group: David R. Maas
Managing Editor: Jill Anderson
Senior Editor and Project Leader: Steven Hauge
Creative Director: Brad Springer
Photo Editor and Project Manager: Angela Hartwell
Director, Production Services: Kim Gerber
Production Manager: Helga Thielen
Production Staff: Laura Hokkanen, Stephanie Barakos
Cover Photo: courtesy of Realtree Camouflage
Contributing Photographers: Charles J. Alsheimer, Mike Barlow/Windigo Images, Toby Bridges, Denver Bryan, Bill Buckley/The Green Agency, Gary Clancy, Michael H. Francis, Donald M. Jones, Mark Kayser, Bill Kinney, Lance Krueger, Lon Lauber, Bill Lea, Stephen W. Maas, Bill Marchel, Mark Raycroft, Dusan Smetana, Bill Vaznis/ The Green Agency

Contributing Individuals: Gary Clancy, John Collins, Mark Drury, Tim Dugas, Betty Lou Fegely, Tom Fegely, Peter Fiduccia, Carl Ganter, Jay Gregory, David Hale, Brad Harris, Dave Henderson, Steve Hornady, Bill Jordan, Mike Jordan, Harold Knight, Jerry Martin, Don Oster, Dan Perez, Stan Potts, Dave Samuel, Jim Shockey, John Sloan, Larry Weishuhn

Printed on American paper by: R. R. Donnelley & Sons Co.
10 9 8 7 6 5 4 3 2 1

Library of Congress Cataloging-in-Publication Data

Bridges, Toby.
    Hunting record-book bucks : deer hunting's top whitetail experts reveal their secrets for success / by Toby Bridges
        p. cm. -- (Complete hunter)
    ISBN 1-58923-039-6
    1. White-tailed deer hunting. I. Title. II. Complete hunter (Creative Publishing International)

SK301 .B73 2002
799.2'7652--dc21
                                        2001059882

CONTENTS

Introduction

As Dan Rederick of South Dakota knows, hunting record-book bucks takes dedication and hard work.

For the dedicated trophy whitetail hunter, these are the "best of times and the worst of times." Never before in history have there been as many whitetails in North America as there are right now. Estimates of current population levels range from 20 to 22 million deer. In fact, many professional whitetail managers believe there are more deer roaming this country today than when the first European immigrants stepped ashore nearly 400 years ago.

The situation hasn't always been so bright for the deer, or for those who enjoy pursuing them. During the first half of the 1900s, the whitetail deer was nearly lost across much of the United States. For instance, in my home state of Illinois there were as few as 1,000 deer remaining statewide at the end of the 1930s. The once abundant whitetails weren't lost to "sport hunting." Instead, the deer were "shot out" by market and subsistence hunters, either for a source of income or to feed a hungry family. This nation was in the grip of hard times during the Great Depression, and any deer that wandered too close to the muzzle of a rifle usually became meat for the pot. Few families were concerned about newly enacted game laws protecting wildlife. Most simply worried about finding their next meal.

Out of this period also came the salvation for the nation's deer herd. Many conservation programs were enacted in order to put Americans back to work and do something for the country's dwindling wildlife populations, including the establishment of many early national and state wildlife refuges. And during these hard times many marginal farms were abandoned, left to revert back to the thick brush and undergrowth wildlife needed for cover. Following World War II, stronger wildlife laws were enacted – and enforced. Due to these efforts many wildlife species made a remarkable comeback, including the whitetail deer.

Today wildlife managers are faced with a new problem. There are now simply too many deer across most of the country. In the Midwestern hardwoods where I roamed as a boy chasing squirrels with a .22 rifle, it was rare to even see a deer track during the early 1960s. Now there are an estimated 45 to 60 deer per square mile inhabiting these same woods. Wildlife professionals would feel more comfortable if the population density was 25 to 30 deer per square mile. Illinois is now home to about 750,000 whitetails, and despite long, liberal seasons, the herd continues to grow in many regions of the state. And just about everywhere this magnificent game animal is found, the story is the same, with some of the highest deer densities often found right inside city limits or suburban areas.

This abundance of deer has resulted in new and longer seasons. In many states the bowhunter can keep after whitetails for 3 months or longer. Most states now also schedule at least one muzzleloader season, often two, while modern firearms seasons are generally longer and may allow the hunter to harvest bonus deer. Where hunters just 20 to 30 years ago were allowed to harvest a single whitetail each season, liberal bag limits may permit harvesting three, four, five and sometimes more deer each year. And to do so, more and more hunters have become "three-season" hunters, taking full advantage of the general firearms season, the muzzleloader season and the archery deer season.

In geographic areas known for producing record-book-class bucks, much of the prime deer habitat has been leased by outfitters. A first-class 5-day fully guided hunt in some of these areas will top $4,000, putting these hunts out of reach for the majority of hunters. Where local farmers once welcomed local hunters to help keep the deer numbers in check, many of these lands are now closed to area residents. Outfitters will often pay $20 to $30 per acre to lease productive big-buck habitat, and may run just 10 to 12 hunters on a given 500-acre farm during the course of an entire fall. Landowners simply cannot ignore that quality big-buck hunting now has a value, that there are trophy-minded hunters willing to pay the price.

Where prime deer hunting is found, small groups of hunters or clubs are also becoming more and more commonplace. Four or five hunting buddies may even pool their cash to purchase a huntable tract of deer country. To insure quality hunting for themselves, these groups or clubs will generally close their lands to local hunters. Whether the ground has been leased or purchased, the hunter without the big bucks to spend to hunt big bucks will continue to find fewer and fewer places to hunt.

On the positive side, as landowners realize profits from the deer hunting conducted on their properties, many are doing more to manage for quality deer. Most sizeable farms in good deer country now include either specially planted food plots for the deer, or crops that have been set aside and left for the wildlife. Unfortunately, managing for "buck-only" hunting isn't sound deer management. Studies have revealed that of the deer harvested by hunters on a fully outfitted hunt, between 70 and 80 percent are bucks. Unless does are harvested as well, it doesn't take long before the buck-to-doe ratio really gets out of whack.

The current emphasis on harvesting a true trophy-class whitetail buck is nothing short of astounding. An entire leading segment of the hunting industry has been established around hunting big whitetail bucks. At major outdoor industry trade shows, the number of products designed specifically for the trophy-whitetail hunter easily equals the number of products being marketed for hunting all other big game. Many of these products have a place in the deer woods, while some amount to little more than gimmicks. However, none can guarantee the success the advertising and promotional hype may lead the hunter to believe. In the end, success comes from good hunting and honed woods savvy.

In the following pages, *Hunting Record-Book Bucks* brings to you the guarded tactics, techniques, how-to details and whitetail-hunting knowledge of more than a dozen of today's most recognized deer hunting experts. The information they share is sure to help you the next time you match wits with a wary trophy whitetail.

–*Toby Bridges*

Equipment
FOR
RECORD-BOOK
BUCKS

Selecting the Correct
Centerfire Deer Rifle or Shotgun

by Toby Bridges

Where legal, the firearm of choice by serious whitetail hunters has long been a quality centerfire rifle capable of putting a 130- to 200-grain bullet exactly where it needs to go at 100, 200 or 300 yards, depending on the whitetail habitat being hunted. However, the majority of whitetail deer hunters in the United States live and hunt in areas with shotgun-only restrictions.

In the following pages we'll take a look at some of the more popular centerfire deer-hunting cartridges and their capabilities. The ballistics and bullet selections detailed should help you to make a more informed choice if you are looking at buying a new deer rifle, or to better realize the performance you can expect from a favorite rifle you already own. This chapter will also take a look at the more recent developments in shotguns built expressly for shooting slugs and the vast improvements in the slugs themselves. Hunting deer today with a slug-shooting shotgun doesn't pose the same handicap that trying to take a big-game animal with grandpa's hand-me-down cylinder-bore quail gun once did. Within their effective range, some of these shotguns and slug loads are surprisingly accurate and effective on deer.

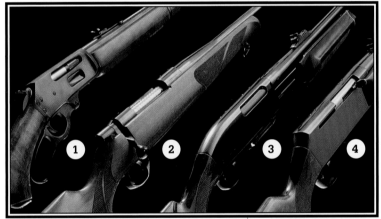

Centerfire Deer Rifles

Not all centerfire rifle cartridges have been developed equally – or with the same purpose in mind. When it comes to centerfire deer rifles a hunter can choose from basically five different types of actions: the bolt-action repeater, the semi-auto repeater, the pump-action repeater, the lever-action repeater and the single-shot. (The majority of the latter are built with a "break-open" type action.)

Within each action category, you'll find a variety of models from various rifle manufacturers. Due to the strength of some action designs, some of these rifles will be available only chambered for cartridges that are compatible with that particular action or design.

POPULAR ACTIONS include: (1) lever action, which chambers and ejects cartridges by means of a lever behind the trigger guard; (2) bolt action, in which the user locks the cartridge in place by moving the bolt forward and downward, much like a door bolt; (3) pump or slide action, which the user chambers and ejects by sliding the forearm back and forth; (4) semi-automatic or autoloader action, in which the chamber ejects automatically after each shot.

The range needs of deer hunters that hunt primarily in one type of cover will vary as much as personal taste. For instance, two hunters who hunt the thick brush of Michigan's Upper Peninsula may favor two completely different types of rifles and cartridges. One may opt for a short, fast handling lever-action that has open sights and is chambered for a brush-busting caliber like the .444 Marlin. The other may prefer a semi-auto rifle in .30/06 loaded with hefty 180- or 220-grain bullets, and have the rifle topped with a 1.5- to 5-power variable scope. Both are excellent choices for short-range shooting in heavy cover.

To clearly identify some of today's more popular whitetail cartridges, and the application (terrain) for which they are most suited, they have been broken down into three different categories – short range, medium range and long range.

Short-Range Deer Rifles

(50 to 150 yards effective range)

.30/30 WINCHESTER – This "old-timer" has been around since 1895, first chambered in the then-brand-new Winchester Model 94 lever-action rifle. It holds the distinction of being the first American smokeless-powder sporting-rifle cartridge. And since its early popularity during the late 1890s, millions of rifles have been chambered for the .30/30 Winchester cartridge. More than 10 million Winchester Model 94 and Marlin 336 lever-action rifles have been sold, and the majority of these were chambered for this cartridge. Additionally, dozens of other lever-action, bolt-action and single-shot rifles have been offered in .30/30 caliber.

Today the cartridge remains one of the top five sellers when it comes to commercially loaded ammunition. It's not because the .30/30 Winchester is such a powerhouse for taking deer and other big game, but because so many rifles have been chambered for it in the past and are still in use. Winchester, Remington and Federal, plus a few other smaller ammunition makers, continue to offer rounds for the old "thirty-thirty." Ammunition loaded with 150- or 170-grain round-nosed bullets tends to be about equally popular, but for the short-range 50 to 150 yards where this cartridge performs best, the 170-grain loads offer more knockdown power.

Winchester's "Silvertip" Super-X 170-grain bullet leaves the muzzle at 2,200 f.p.s., generating 1,827 foot-pounds of energy. At 100 yards, the slow-moving bullet hits with just 1,355 foot-pounds of

remaining energy, and out at 200 yards the bullet hits a whitetail with only 989 foot-pounds of knockdown power. Sighted dead on at 100 yards, this load impacts about 0.6 inches high at 50 yards, and nearly 9 inches low at 200 yards. Considering the quick drop-off of remaining energy and excessive drop-out at 200 yards and farther, the .30/30 Winchester should be considered a 50- to 150-yard-effective deer rifle.

.35 REMINGTON – This cartridge was first introduced in 1908 for the Remington Model 8 semi-automatic rifle. In the past, other models have also been chambered for the .35 Remington, including several early Remington slide-action rifles, the Remington Model 30 bolt-action and the Winchester Model 70 bolt-action rifles. For years, Marlin has offered their Model 336 in this cartridge as an alternative to the .30/30 Winchester. It is one of very few rifles still offered in the caliber.

Winchester, Remington and Federal all offer cartridges loaded with a 200-grain round-nosed bullet. Factory loads generally put the 200-grain bullet out of the muzzle at around 2,100 f.p.s. with right at 1,925 foot-pounds of muzzle energy. Out at 100 yards, the bullet hits with some 1,300 foot-pounds of deer-taking energy, but drops to only about 850 foot-pounds at 200 yards. Sighted to hit dead on at 100 yards, the load generally prints about a half-inch high at 50 yards and 3½ inches low at 150 yards. Out at 200 yards, the bullet is nearly 11 inches down from point of aim. The .35 Remington is another good 50- to 150-yard whitetail rifle.

.44 REMINGTON MAGNUM – The popularity of the .44 Remington Magnum cartridge as a handgun cartridge destined it to eventually become a long-gun cartridge as well. During the heyday of lever-action rifles during the late 1880s, it was common for shooters to own both rifle and pistol that utilized the same cartridge, and calibers like the old .38/40 and .44/40 Winchester cartridges were widely used in both sidearms and lever-action rifles.

Out of a long-barreled revolver like the Smith & Wesson Model 29 or Ruger Redhawk, the .44 Remington Magnum has won a real reputation for being a powerhouse. When fired from a carbine or rifle with an 18- to 24-inch barrel, the cartridge offers even better ballistics. Through the 1960s and 1970s, quite a few Ruger .44 Magnum semi-auto carbines found their way into the deer woods, while Winchester and Marlin lever-action rifles in that caliber have become popular.

Out of a 20-inch barrel, Winchester Super-X .44 Remington Magnum ammunition with a 240-grain jacketed hollow-point bullet is good for 1,760 f.p.s. and 1,650 foot-pounds of energy at the muzzle. At 100 yards, energy levels are down to 988 foot-pounds, indicating that any .44 Magnum rifle or carbine is basically a 100-yard maximum effective range deer gun. Sighted to hit on at 50 yards, the Winchester factory round will impact 2¾ inches low at 100 yards and just over 10 inches down at 150 yards, where the bullet hits with only around 640 foot-pounds of energy – hardly enough to insure a clean kill.

.444 MARLIN – Whitetail hunters looking for a more powerful .44-caliber short-range deer rifle with lots of knockdown power and the ability to bust its way through brush should take a closer look at the rifles chambered for the .444 Marlin. This cartridge was first developed for the Marlin Model 336 lever-action rifles and introduced in 1964. Today Marlin continues to offer this powerful .44 in its line of lever-action rifles, and Winchester is now chambering the Model 94 in the caliber as well.

Remington's 240-grain factory load for the .444 Marlin produces a muzzle velocity of 2,350 f.p.s., while generating 2,924 foot-pounds of energy at the muzzle. At 100 yards, the bullet hits with 1,755 foot-pounds of wallop, and with 1,010 foot-pounds of energy all the way out at 200 yards. Zeroed to hit on at 100 yards, the big bullet would be 3¼ inches low at 150 and nearly 10 inches low at 200 yards. While a hunter may easily learn to compensate for the drop-out at the longer distance, the .444 Marlin is one fine brush-busting 50- to 150-yard deer cartridge.

Medium-Range Deer Rifles
(250 to 300 yards maximum effective range)

.270 WINCHESTER – This has been one of the best-selling deer-hunting cartridges for most of the last 50 years. The .270 Winchester had its debut back in 1925, designed originally for the Winchester Model 54 bolt-action rifle. Today practically every major centerfire rifle maker in the world chambers one or more models for this cartridge.

Most ammunition makers today load 130-, 140- and 150-grain bullets for the .270 Winchester, and while the heavier bullet definitely offers more knockdown power, it seems that the lighter 130- and 140-grain loadings enjoy the greatest popularity. This is likely due to the fact that the .270 Winchester enjoys its greatest popularity in semi-open to open terrain,

where shots are very often out past 200 yards. The lighter bullets offer flatter trajectory.

Federal Cartridge Company loads the 130-grain Nosler Ballistic Tip bullet in its Premium line of centerfire rifle ammunition. At the muzzle, the bullet is good for 3,080 f.p.s., and develops 2,700 foot-pounds of muzzle energy. Out at 100 yards, the bullet hits with 2,325 foot-pounds of energy, 1,890 foot-pounds at 200 yards and 1,700 foot-pounds at 300 yards. In fact, this bullet still hits with around 1,200 foot-pounds of punch all the way out at 500 yards.

The only thing that really keeps the .270 Winchester from being a great choice for shooting out past 300 yards is its trajectory. Zeroed to hit dead on at 100 yards, the 130-grain bullets will normally hit around 1¼ inches low at 200, close to 4 inches down at 250 and around 8¼ inches low out at 300 yards. A good rifle shot with knowledge of ballistics and trajectory can easily learn to compensate for this amount of drop. However, in the next 100 yards after passing the 300-yard mark a 130-grain bullet that left the muzzle of a .270 rifle at just over 3,000 f.p.s. will nosedive to hit more than 21 inches low at 400 yards.

.308 WINCHESTER – Many knowledgeable shooters who have hunted with this cartridge and a number of other popular deer-hunting calibers and have had the opportunity to make a comparison, readily acknowledge the .308 Winchester as one of the finest medium-range cartridges available today. Most ammunition makers offer both 150- and 180-grain loads for rifles of this caliber. While the heavier bullet may enjoy better application where the hunter may encounter light brush and shots under 200 yards, for shots out to 300 yards the lighter 150-grain bullet definitely offers flatter trajectory while still delivering more than ample knockdown power.

Sighted to hit dead on at 100 yards, most factory 150-grain loads leave the muzzle at around 2,820 f.p.s. with 2,648 foot-pounds of energy. At 100 yards, the bullet hits with 1,957 foot-pounds of energy, 1,610 foot-pounds at 200 yards and 1,314 foot-pounds of remaining deer-taking wallop out at 300 yards. A rifle sighted to print this load dead on at 100 yards would be 1.2 inches low at 150, 3.9 inches low at 200 yards and 14 inches down at 300 yards. At 400 yards the bullet would drop a full 28 inches.

.30/06 SPRINGFIELD - America's favorite big-game cartridge actually started life as a U.S. military round. The .30-caliber cartridge was officially adopted in 1906, thus the "06" part of its designation. The first rifle chambered for the caliber was the famed Model 1903 Springfield bolt-action military rifle, while the first sporting rifle to offer a chambering for the cartridge was the Winchester Model 1895 lever-action in 1908. Through most of the past century the .30/06 became one of the most widely used calibers for hunting deer and most other big game. Many experienced big-game hunters still consider it the most versatile big-game cartridge ever introduced.

The versatility stems from the fact that the ammunition is offered in a wide range of bullet weights, and the cartridges can also be hand loaded with bullets from as light as 100 grains to well over 200 grains. The .30/06 can be used on everything from varmints to the biggest of bears. However, for whitetails factory loads with 150- or 180-grain bullets tend to be the most widely used.

Like the .308 Winchester, trajectory becomes the limiting factor for the .30/06 as an honest long-range deer rifle. A factory-loaded Remington cartridge with a 150-grain soft-point Core-Lokt spitzer style bullet leaves the muzzle at 2,910 f.p.s. with 2,820 foot-pounds of energy. At 100 yards, the bullet hits with 2,281 foot-pounds, with 1,827 foot-pounds at 200 yards and 1,445 foot-pounds of punch at 300 yards. Sighted to hit on at 100 yards, the bullet would be 3 inches below point of aim at 200 yards and around 12 inches down at 300 yards. Out at 400 yards, the bullet would impact 26 inches low, but would still have more than 1,100 foot-pounds of energy remaining.

Long-Range Deer Rifles

7MM REMINGTON MAGNUM – Coinciding with the introduction of their new Model 700 series of bolt-action rifles in 1962, Remington Arms Co. also introduced a new belted magnum cartridge – the 7mm Remington Magnum. Today, it has become one of the top five sellers among commercial cartridges. Rifles in this caliber have likewise become extremely popular with today's hunter, especially the shooter looking to extend the effective range of the rifle he or she hunts with.

Factory loads are available with bullets weighing up to 175 grains, which are extremely popular with elk hunters. However, to tap the long-range potential of this cartridge for use on whitetails that may be feeding on the far side of a wide field or crossing a power-line cut 500 yards away, hunters are finding bullets of 140 to 150 grains a more practical choice.

Loaded with 140-grain Nosler Partition bullets, Federal Premium factory centerfire ammunition will push the spire-point bullet from the muzzle at 3,150 f.p.s. with 3,085 foot-pounds of energy. All the way out at 500 yards, this bullet still has more than 1,400 foot-pounds of big-buck-stopping power.

When shooting primarily long range, experienced shooters find that it's best to sight a flat-shooting cartridge like the 7mm Remington Magnum to print dead on at 250 yards. With the Federal 140-grain factory load zeroed at that distance, the bullet

Ballistics Table for the Most Popular Cartridges

Type of Cartridge
(shown actual size)

.270 Winchester – 130 grain

7mm Remington Magnum – 150 grain

.30/30 Winchester – 170 grain

	Range (in yards)			
	100	200	300	400
Energy*	2,225	1,818	1,472	1,180
Trajectory†	+1.8	0.0	–7.4	–21.6
Energy*	2,667	2,196	1,792	1,448
Trajectory†	+1.7	0.0	–7.0	–20.5
Energy*	1,355	989	720	535
Trajectory†	+2.0	–4.8	–25.1	–63.6

*Energy in foot-pounds   †Trajectory in inches above or below line of aim   Note: All cartridges were sighted in at 200 yards except .30/30 (150 yards) and .308 (100 yards).

impacts just 2½ inches high at 100 yards, only 1½ inches high at 200 yards, 3½ inches low at 300 yards, 14½ inches below point of aim at 400 yards, and a full 32 inches low at 500 yards. (A 140-grain .270 Winchester factory load would be around 42 inches below point of aim at 500 yards.)

.300 WINCHESTER MAGNUM – Perhaps as a counter to Remington's powerful long-range 7mm Magnum introduced in 1962, Winchester introduced their belted .300 Magnum in 1963 for the Model 70 bolt-action rifles. The cartridge is basically the .338 Winchester Magnum case necked down to .30 caliber. It has been the most popular .30-caliber magnum cartridge ever introduced, and more rifles have been chambered for it than any other cartridge in its class.

One real advantage of the .300 Winchester Magnum over the 7mm Remington Magnum is that the larger .30-caliber cartridge allows the hunter to shoot a heavier 150-grain bullet at velocities higher than are possible with lighter 140-grain bullets out of rifles chambered for the smaller-belted magnum cartridge. Out of a 24-inch barrel, Winchester's 150-grain Super-X load produces right at 3,300 f.p.s. at the muzzle with more than 3,600 foot-pounds of energy. Downrange at 500 yards, the bullet plows home with more than 1,500 foot-pounds of energy.

Sighted to hit dead on at 250 yards, the bullet will hit just 2 inches high at 100, and 4 inches low at 300 yards. At 400 yards the 150-grain bullet would hit the target around 17 inches below point of aim, and all the way out at 500 yards the .300 Winchester Magnum would put a 150-grain bullet just over 37 inches low.

OTHER MAGNUM LONG-RANGE DEER CARTRIDGES – The 7mm Remington Magnum and .300 Winchester Magnum cartridges are far from being the only suitable "high-velocity" long-range cartridges available. However, they have been the most successful of the commercial magnum cartridges. Roy Weatherby began playing around with necked-down versions of the .300 Holland & Holland case during the early- to mid-1940s to develop the forerunners of his hot Weatherby Magnum cartridges. His .270 Weatherby Magnum takes a 130-grain bullet to nearly 3,400 f.p.s., while the 7mm Weatherby Magnum pushes a 140-grain bullet out of the muzzle at more than 3,300 f.ps. and a .300 Weatherby Magnum tops 3,500 f.p.s. with a 150-grain bullet. Downrange performance is just as impressive and trajectories out to 500 yards extremely flat.

Now we have the new Lazzeroni cartridges establishing new speed and trajectory records. The Lazzeroni 7.21 FIREHAWK gets a 140-grain bullet out of the muzzle at 3,480 f.p.s., with less than 24 inches of drop from muzzle to 500 yards. The 7.82 WARBIRD takes a 150-grain bullet to an astounding 3,680 f.p.s. at the muzzle, with 4,512 foot-pounds of energy. Way out there at 500 yards, the bullet drops just 22 inches and hammers a whitetail with 2,188 foot-pounds of remaining energy.

Type of Cartridge
(shown actual size)

.30/06 Springfield – 150 grain

.308 Win. – 150 grain

.300 Win. Mag. – 180 grain

	Range (in yards)			
	100	200	300	400
Energy*	2,281	1,827	1,445	1,131
Trajectory†	+2.1	0.0	−8.5	−25.0
Energy*	1,957	1,610	1,314	1,050
Trajectory†	0.0	-3.9	−14.0	−28.0
Energy*	3,011	2,578	2,196	1,859
Trajectory†	+1.9	0.0	−7.3	−20.9

High-Performance Slug-Shooting Shotguns

Back when most states began establishing "shotgun-only" regulations for hunting deer statewide or zoning some parts of the state "shotgun only" due to dense human populations, range was the basis for the decisions of most game departments. Where deer and human development were in close proximity, often sharing the same 40-acre woodlot, game departments felt that safety dictated hunters should not be allowed to hunt deer with centerfire rifles with long-range capabilities. Shotguns and slug loads with an effective range of 100 to 125 yards seemed a safer alternative.

Unfortunately, the vast majority of deer hunters faced with using shot-

guns and slugs through the 1950s, 1960s, 1970s and most of the 1980s were, for the most part, hunting deer with the very same shotgun they used to hunt everything from rabbits to waterfowl. The vast majority of the shotguns used then featured every choke constriction imaginable, from full to cylinder bore. And a very high percentage of those hunters who head out today to do a little deer hunting in a "shotgun state" still rely on the same very inadequate shotguns. Instead of making one or two precisely placed shots to harvest the deer they shoot at, many often go through a box of slugs and never cut a hair. All of those slugs end up somewhere, which sort of shoots down the safety claims by governing game departments.

Fortunately, there continues to be a growing number of shotgun models designed expressly for the whitetail-deer hunter. Not only do these models generally come with a set of adjustable "rifle-type" hunting sights, but most of these so-called deer-hunting shotguns now feature a rifled bore for vastly improved performance with slugs of superior design.

Shotgun slugs of 40 to 50 years ago were little more than hunks of lead weighing anywhere from 1/2 to 1 ounce, depending on the gauge of the shotgun from which they were shot. The slugs were one of two types or designs. The American slug design, which was introduced around 1936, was a bore-sized projectile that featured a deep hollow base, similar to the big Minie bullets dating from the Civil War. The other type of slug is often referred to as the German style slug, which was a solid lead slug featuring a very blunt nose and often a felt wad attached to the base by a screw.

Except for very few custom-built slug-shooting shotguns, even those shotguns sold as deer-hunting shotguns did not feature rifled bores. Accuracy with the early slug designs was dependent on raised rifling fins formed onto the outer surface of the slug; thus they were often referred to as rifled slugs.

These rifling rays or fins gripped the smooth bore of the shotgun and supposedly caused the slug to spin on its axis, helping to stabilize the massive lead projectile in flight. Most deer-hunting shotguns, such as the old Ithaca "Deerslayer" of the period, featured a cylinder bore barrel to keep from constricting the slug so tightly that they deformed or totally removed the rifling from the slug. Still, most shotgun hunters of the past shot the slugs through modified and full-choke constrictions.

Today's newer deer-hunting shotguns are much better suited for pursuing close-cover whitetails. And to make slug hunting more effective, these guns require a completely different type of slug, one that features an undersized projectile that travels encased in a plastic sabot down a rifled bore. The sabot protects the projectile from being damaged as it is pushed down the barrel by the burning powder charge and transfers the spin of the shallow rifling to the projectile. Almost at the instant the sabot and slug leave the muzzle, the sabot peels or drops away from the projectile.

Cutaway of an early saboted bullet

Deer-hunting shotguns like the bolt-action Savage Model 210F Slug Gun, semi-auto Remington Model 11-87 Premier Deer Gun, semi-auto Browning Gold Deer Gun, and pump Ithaca Deerslayer II shotguns are capable of shooting three-shot hundred-yard groups that can be just 1 inch center-to-center. And thanks to the improved performance of modern saboted slugs, some of these guns and loads are now honest 150- to 200-yard deer guns.

The Federal Premium Barnes Expander slugs are a great example of the thought that has gone into the design of today's saboted slugs. This deadly deer-hunting shotgun load features a saboted all-copper Barnes projectile (similar to the Expander MZ bullet Barnes packages for the muzzleloading hunter). The 3-inch and 2 3/4-inch 12-gauge slug loads come with a 438-grain deeply hollow-pointed bullet, while the 20-gauge loading features a 325-grain all-copper hollow-point. The 3-inch magnum load gets the bullet out of the muzzle of a 24-inch barrel at 1,525 f.p.s. with 2,260 foot-pounds of energy. At 100 yards the Barnes bullet hits with 1,560 foot-pounds of knockdown power, and with 1,325 foot-pounds at 125 yards.

Even the little 20-gauge Barnes slug load is good for 1,450 f.p.s. at the muzzle with 1,515 foot-pounds of energy at 100 yards. Zeroed to hit on at 100 yards, any of the Federal saboted slugs with Barnes all-copper bullets will impact no more than 2.3 inches high at 50 yards.

A growing number of new saboted slug loads are even surpassing this kind of performance. Many of the improved bullet/slug designs now feature ballistic coefficients exceeding .200, which contributes to downrange performance, especially retained velocities and energy levels. Some of the early hourglass-shaped saboted bullets (below) had a ballistic coefficient of only around .100, while the older "Foster" style slugs dating from the 1950s and earlier had a ballistic coefficient of around .060. Some of today's hotter saboted slug loads are capable of generating more than 3,000 foot-pounds of whitetail-taking energy at the muzzle.

Remember, the main reason why so many game departments went to "shotgun-only" regulations 50 or so years ago was for safety. The shotguns and slugs of the period did offer limited 100- to 125-yard range. Today's shotguns and slugs have changed all of that. It's not uncommon to now hear a hunter boast of taking his buck at 200 yards with a saboted slug fired from a scoped shotgun with a rifled bore (which actually makes it a rifle). Whether most hunters can pull off a shot like that or not, many are trying. Maybe it's time for some game departments to reconsider their "shotgun-only" restrictions and look at allowing the short-range centerfire rifle cartridges covered earlier in this chapter. Precise shot placement with a rifle would mean far fewer slugs being fired, resulting in a safer hunting environment.

The poor performance of early slugs and the less-than-adequate shotguns most were shot from resulted in many lost whitetails. If you are faced with shotgun regulations where you hunt and are still shooting old-style slugs out of your grandpa's or dad's old cylinder-bore quail gun, maybe it's time you sprung for a shotgun designed specifically to shoot slugs. You owe it to yourself and to the deer you hunt. One thing is for certain, your odds of hanging your tag on a good buck will improve dramatically. 🦌

CENTERFIRE RIFLE: A MATTER OF CHOICE

by Toby Bridges

The following renowned deer hunters could be envied by the average deer hunter since they often have the opportunity to spend most of each fall hunting big game. This is primarily due to their professions. Some are noted outdoor writers who make their living by writing about shooting and hunting; others work with the development and marketing of the fine hunting products we now enjoy.

Because of their close relationships with the outdoor industry, any of them could hunt with just about any centerfire rifle they choose. Here is a look at their favored choices.

Betty Lou Fegely, *Outdoor Writer* – "I shot my first whitetail with a rifle chambered for the .30/30 Winchester. Since, I've graduated up to a Remington Model 7 in the 7mm-08 caliber, which I doubt I'll ever give up. Weighing just over 6 pounds, it's the perfect choice for the young hunter or woman. That's not to say that men shouldn't consider it. The 140-grain load traveling at 2,800 feet per second is a dandy flat-shooter and may well be the "perfect" cartridge for medium game, although I did cleanly drop a 500-pound Colorado cinnamon bear with it."

Mike Jordan, *Public Relations Manager, Winchester-Olin* – "I prefer a good bolt-action rifle like the Winchester Model 70 chambered for the .270 Winchester, topped with a high quality 3x9 or 4x14 power scope. The bullet I shoot depends on the terrain and cover being hunted. In Missouri, where most shots will be well inside of 200 yards, I prefer a 150-grain bullet. In open country, such as that in Wyoming, I go with the 130-grain loads for the flatter trajectory."

Steve Hornady, *President, Hornady Manufacturing Company* – "I really don't have a "favorite" rifle or caliber, but one I hunt with regularly is the Browning A-Bolt in .30/06. Shooting our Hornady Light Magnum loads with a 165-grain bullet, the rifle is a tack driver and extremely effective on whitetails. Well-placed shots will drop deer where they stand!"

Tom Fegely, *Outdoor Writer and Betty Lou's husband* – "For years, I hunted almost exclusively with a Remington Model 700 in .30/06. And I took quite a few whitetails with that rifle. However, the .270 Winchester has now become my personal favorite, and I've taken whitetails with rifles in this caliber from Texas north into Canada.

"The caliber seems to be inherently accurate, and with 130- to 150-grain bullets will anchor any whitetail that is properly hit."

Don Oster, *Outdoor Writer and Book Author* – "I've only owned two real deer rifles, both of which are Remington Model 700s. One is chambered for the old .264 Winchester Magnum, the other for the .300 Winchester Magnum. I guess you could call me a fan of long-range shooting, and for whitetails I would opt for the .300 Winchester Magnum with 150-grain loads. I have my rifle topped with a good 3- to 9-power scope and when conditions are perfect, I have no reservation of taking a 400-yard shot. The rifle is always capable of doing the job."

SLUG MASTER

by Dave Henderson

Dave Henderson

Nothing spurs technology into motion faster than the profit motive and competition. With the increased amount of whitetail habitat now designated "shotgun only," a growing number of deer hunters must now use a shotgun with slugs to hunt their favorite deer woods. This has created a growing demand for improved deer shotguns and slugs.

In just the last decade there have been some significant changes made in the designs and effectiveness of the slugs being used. In fact, since the early 1990s slug shooting has come farther than it had during the entire previous century.

Those rifling grooves or fins that were either swaged or cast into the soft lead of older Foster-style slugs were more for sales appeal than for function. This "rifling" on the slug did little to actually spin the slugs. It was the nose-heavy design of early slugs, even the German Brenneke solid slugs, that stabilized them in flight. Accuracy out of most shotguns was poor at best, limiting the effectiveness of the average shotgun

with slug loads to around 50 or 75 yards.

Sabot slugs have improved greatly since they first hit the market back in the 1970s. Most designs still rely heavily on the nose-forward weight for stability, while the spin of a rifled bore does improve accuracy. Just as important have been the improved velocities and higher energy levels.

Velocity has become the new objective in the slug-shooting community. Some of the newer slug loads are pushing the 2,000 f.p.s. mark. What does the increased velocity of the new designs mean in terms of trajectory? Well, the rule of thumb for a 100-yard zero with past sabot slugs at about 1,450 f.ps. was to center them at least 2.5 inches high at 50 yards. In my experience, the new Hornady and Lightfield loads need only be 1 inch high at 50 to zero at 100. In fact, I printed the Winchester Partition Golds 2 inches high at 50 for a 150-yard zero.

These are shotgun slugs we're talking about, but with performance that rivals the .45-70 centerfire rifle.

Thanks to modern technology, women and young hunters using bows with 45- to 50-pound draw weights can easily harvest big-bodied whitetails.

Bowhunting
for Record-Book Bucks

with Dan Perez

Noted bowhunting authority Dan Perez makes his home in the rolling hills of Pike County, Illinois, a region that has built a deserving reputation as one of the top big whitetail-buck-producing areas in the United States today. Within minutes of his back door, this ardent bowhunter can be sitting in one of the many tree-stands he hangs well before and throughout the entire 3-month archery season. And from October first on into early January, here is where you are likely to find him most mornings and evenings, when he's not on the road fulfilling the responsibilities of his job as a regional sales manager for Precision Shooting Equipment (PSE).

This woods-savvy archer will be one of the first to endorse the many techniques and tactics covered by the other respected whitetail-hunting experts who have shared valuable hunting information in this book. Even so, this very successful bowhunter, who has harvested dozens of Pope-&-Young-class whitetail bucks, feels that the number-one tip he could share with you is to stress how important it is to rely on the best quality bow and accessories a hunter can afford.

"It's amazing how much time and effort some hunters spend to locate a good buck, scouting and patterning, selecting stand locations, and putting in long hours in those stands at the right times of the season, only to hunt with mismatched equipment or equipment that may even be less than adequate," states Perez.

When choosing a hunting bow, and for the most part we're talking about a modern compound bow, today's hunter has an unbelievable selection from which to choose the model that best fits his or her needs or budget. Perez is a very equipment-conscious archer and feels that the beginning bowhunter on a tight budget is still more apt to find a model that fills the bill when considering those bows that fall into the mid-price range. He points out that "consumers get what they pay for," and that the cost of a bow generally reflects the overall quality, design, feel, handling characteristics, and most importantly, the performance of the bow.

"In the past, I've had to cut corners and buy something below a top-of-the-line model, only to later wish I had spent a little more to get all of the features and performance I was really looking for," he claims.

Perez acknowledges that compound bow technology has come a long way over just the past decade, and that current models are easily the finest bows ever manufactured. The following are a few pointers he shares with the hunter looking to purchase a first hunting bow, or the bowhunter wanting to move up to a newer, more efficient model.

His first bit of advice is that a hunter concentrate on those models that offer at least 65 percent let-off in draw weight. In other words, when the bow is at full draw, the hunter is holding back only about a third or less of the actual poundage of the draw weight. For instance, a bow that has a 65-pound draw weight would require about 20 to 25 pounds of effort to hold the arrow at full draw. Perez says this not only allows the hunter to shoot a heavier poundage bow using less muscle, it also allows the hunter to keep the arrow at full draw until the deer offers the perfect shot. Bows with this much or more let-off are also more enjoyable to shoot for longer lengths of time, and since they fatigue the archer less, most entry-level archers can become proficient with the bow in noticeably less time than with models offering a considerably lower percentage of let-off.

Dan states emphatically that a hunter must be "comfortable" with a bow before he or she will ever reach a high level of proficiency with it. Not only must the grip of the bow fit comfortably in the hand, but the draw length must be correct for the individual shooter and the draw weight within the hunter's ability to bring the bow to full draw without having to exert exaggerated effort. He points out that the latter can become a real problem when hunting in cold-weather conditions. If a hunter can barely draw the bow during warm-weather practice sessions, the weight is probably too much for that individual. When temperatures plunge, drawing a heavy bow can become impossible.

Today's compound bows are not only getting shorter,

most models are getting lighter as well. Our seasoned bowhunting expert readily admits that a featherweight model may be a delight to pack in to those distant stand sites, but adds that a heavier bow can help steady your hold – especially when you're holding on a nice buck and your heart is trying to jump through your throat! However, keep in mind that accessory weights and stabilizers allow the hunter to add weight to a light bow, but an overly heavy bow will always be an overly heavy bow.

A lot of emphasis is now placed on arrow speed. Quite a few current bow models claim speeds exceeding 300 f.p.s. Perez currently shoots and hunts with one of the PSE "Mach Series" models, which launches a full-length broadhead-tipped carbon arrow at around 275 f.p.s. He switched to carbon arrows during recent bow seasons, mostly because of their precise weight and straightness. This bowhunter insists on shooting the straightest possible arrow shafts, and feels that it is much easier to have precise, straight arrows with the newer carbon materials than it is with aluminum shafts.

"With just minimal use during practice, it is possible to affect the straightness of an aluminum arrow, and being only six or so thousandths out of tolerance will affect an arrow's flight and point of impact. This is especially true of broadheads. And that's why I have made the switch to carbon arrows – they're either straight or they're broken! There's no guessing. And they are definitely a lot tougher than what many bowhunters claim," remarks Dan.

While he shoots a 70-pound-draw-weight bow, he says he certainly doesn't need that much poundage, not with today's more efficient compound models. This bowhunter consistently fills his tags with light carbon arrows, matched with light 90-grain Muzzy broadheads, and shoots fully through every deer he's taken with the set-up. He feels that most of the current compound bows set at 60-pound draw weight easily outperform older models which may have had 10 to 15 pounds of additional draw weight. He attributes the improved performance to "smarter designs" that call upon the cams to produce much of the arrow speed and energy. Many of the older compound models relied largely on the thrust of the limbs to transfer the power of the bow to the arrow.

Just 10 or so years ago, many bowhunters felt that if they wanted speed, then they had to concentrate on only those bows which featured two or twin cams. And the thinking was that the more radical the cam, the faster the speed. Often the trade-off

was less consistent accuracy, more bow jump and the ongoing effort of keeping the bow well tuned. However, those bows that featured only one single cam on the lower limb, then an idler wheel on the upper limb, built a reputation for being easier to keep in tune, but also slower. Thanks to advances in technology, Perez sees very little difference in the performance of "two-cam" and "single-cam" bows today. It has simply become a matter of personal choice.

Perez feels that two of the biggest mistakes made by many bowhunters is to shoot a heavier poundage bow than they can physically handle well enough to shoot consistently, and to install accessories that may be totally wrong for the bow or for the shooter. He says, for instance, that release aids should be chosen when matching the bow and arrow length to the shooter's own draw length. The design and manner in which the release attaches to the string can affect draw length, and likewise determine the length of arrows for optimum arrow flight. Another example of matching the relationship of one accessory to another is the installation of a fiber-optic sight and a string "peep" sight. If the diameter of the fiber-optic pin is too large, the hunter may not be able to see around it well enough when sighting through the tiny hole in the "peep" to sight on the target, whether it's a 3-D deer target or the real thing.

"A well-established archery pro shop is the best place for the beginning bowhunter to get himself or herself properly equipped. Sure, it often costs a little more than buying from a discount store, but the services offered by these archery experts are added insurance that you'll be hunting with a bow, arrows and accessories that have been properly matched. And this usually means that you'll be a lot happier with how the rig shoots and how it performs when you get that long-awaited shot at a good whitetail buck," he advises.

Equipment has definitely changed since the days when Dan's father cashed in three "S&H Green Stamp" books to get him his first recurve bow nearly 40 years ago. Since taking his first whitetail with a bow as a teenager during the mid-1960s, he has harvested more than 170 whitetail deer with well-placed arrows. During his more than 35 years of hunting deer with a bow, Perez has hunted with just about every kind of archery equipment imaginable, always striving to improve his odds with a better bow . . . better arrows . . . better broadheads . . . or better accessories with each new season.

"It's the only way to feel confident that I'll make

the most of every new opportunity to harvest another good buck!" claims this very accomplished bowhunter.

Gearing Up for a Successful Season

Since the introduction and early acceptance of the so-called compound bow during the late 1960s and early 1970s, there have been continual improvements in the design and performance of these bows. They have become the bow of choice among today's bowhunters. In fact, according to recent archery industry statistics, as many as 95 percent of all bowhunters in the United States now hunt with a compound bow.

Many bowhunters have never even shot a traditional longbow or recurve bow. For most, a modern compound was their first bow, and the vast majority of bowhunters never turn to traditional archery equipment. In recent years, though, there has been a resurgence of interest in shooting and hunting with long and recurve bows. Still, these historically minded bowhunters make up only about 5 percent of the estimated 3 1/2 million archery hunters in the country today.

The number of compound-bow makers and the selection of models currently available can be astonishing to the archer looking to purchase that first hunting bow, even to the point of being scary. Here we'll take a look at the variations and features from which the buyer must choose.

Cams

Early compound designs relied as much on the flex of the limbs as they did the mechanics of the "eccentric wheels," or cams, located at the ends of the limbs to transfer the power of the bow to the arrow. For nearly two decades during the 1970s and 1980s, all

compound bows produced in this country were manufactured under a licensing agreement from the patent holder. Consequently few makers strayed from the original design, and practically every bow produced during that period offered cams that tended to provide the shooter with 30 to 40 percent let-off of the draw weight. Bows of the day typically produced arrow speeds of 200 to 220 f.p.s.

The competition among manufacturers for the dollars today's bowhunter has to spend on a new bow has been awfully good to archery, especially when it comes to the advanced technology now found in today's newer bow models. Now free from patent restraints, bow makers have taken the compound to the pinnacle of perfection. And many of these improvements can be found in the shapes or designs of the cams at the end of the limbs, or maybe at the end of only one limb.

So-called soft cams are often referred to as energy wheels since many are nearly perfectly round in shape, much like the eccentric wheels found on early compound models. Today's soft cam, however, exhibits a little more thought in its design. The string rides on a round lobe extending from the side of the wheel, while the cable rides on an oval-shaped lobe on the opposite

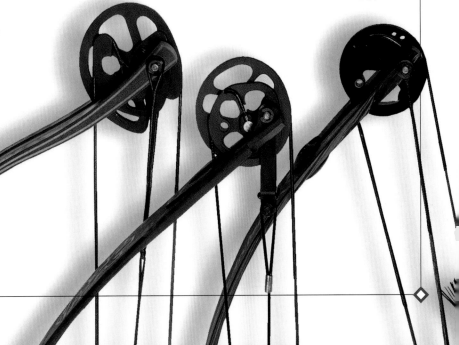

Cam variations include the soft cam (right), medium cam (center) and hard cam (left).

side of the wheel, or cam. The design offers the shooter an exceptionally smooth draw, and delivers more speed and power than earlier wheels with fully rounded lobes on both sides. Even so, soft-cam bows generally do not deliver the speed or power offered by more radical cam designs.

Medium cams feature oval- or oblong-shaped lobes on both the string and cable sides of the cam. The design allows the bow, at full draw, to develop greater energy storage and more effectively transfers this energy from the cable to the string, then on to the arrow. The oval shape of the lobes found on medium-cam bows are moderately out of round, and bows with cams of this design generally still offer an easy, smooth draw.

The most radical design is found with cams of the so-called hard-cam type. With these cams the lobes found on each side of the wheel become more elliptical in shape. While the radical shape does allow the bow to store and produce greater energy levels, along with faster arrow speed, bows with cams of this design become more difficult to bring to full draw. The shooter must be able to "roll over" the cams in a shorter, initial stage of bringing the bow string rearward. This sudden peak of the draw weight can make it even more difficult to draw the bow when hunting during extremely cold weather conditions. However, one benefit of shooting a bow with hard cams is that they do store greater energy, allowing the bowhunter shooting a 60-pound-pull bow to get basically the same arrow speed, trajectory and penetration as a soft- or medium-cam bow having 10 or more pounds of draw weight.

Many early compound designs featured wheels, or cams, at the ends of each limb, then commonly relied on another set of "pulley-type" wheels attached to or near the riser for stringing an often complicated system of cables. By the 1980s, most compound designs incorporated only the cams at the end of each limb, a design that is likely still the most popular. However, gaining on the two-cam bows in popularity have been the solo-cam models that, just as the name implies, feature only one cam, usually at the end of the lower limb. At the end of the other limb is simply a perfectly round and centered wheel known as an idler wheel that accommodates the bowstring and turns as the bow is pulled to full draw and the bottom cam rotates to create the force of the bow. Bows of solo-cam design have won a reputation for being easier to keep in tune, for being quieter than two-cam bows, and for offering a smooth, easy draw.

One other type of compound bow that has been manufactured in limited quantities over the past several decades is often referred to as the lever-action design. Instead of cams at the ends of each limb, bows of this type feature short rocker-type limbs at each end. These are connected by cable to cams that are bracket mounted directly to each end of the riser.

Before selecting a compound hunting bow, hunters must first decide what is most important to them – an easy, smooth draw or speed and power. Bows built with soft cams are generally the easier-to-draw models, while those built with hard cams deliver more energy and arrow speed. Medium-cam bows offer something of a compromise, and consequently tend to be the most popular.

Draw Length and Draw Weight

One's draw length will be determined by an individual's physical characteristics, while maximum draw weight will be determined by the shooter's physical abilities. Generally speaking, it is the length of your arms and the width of your shoulders that largely determine your draw length. And the maximum peak draw weight of the bow you choose will be determined by the amount of weight you can pull back to full draw easily and comfortably.

The hunter who tries to shoot a bow with a draw length that is either too short or too long for him or her will most likely never become consistent with that bow. If the bow does not allow the string to come all the way back, it becomes impossible to lock in on the exact same anchor point for each and every shot. It is possible to overdraw a bow as well, and the hunter who repeatedly shoots a bow from several inches past its intended draw length can eventually damage the bow. Some bows drawn past the set draw length have literally exploded in the hands of the shooter.

Unfortunately, there has always been this macho thing about shooting a heavy-poundage bow. Many hunters who are currently shooting a 70- to 80-pound-draw-weight compound bow would find they can draw a 60-pound-pull bow more easily and probably hit more accurately with the lighter-poundage bow. If you must lift the bow over your head to obtain leverage in order to draw back the string, you're shooting a bow that's too heavy for you.

Fortunately, most bows today come with draw-length adjustments on the cams, making it easier than ever to be shooting a model that's perfectly set for your personal draw length. Also, practically every compound bow currently in production allows some adjustment of the draw weight, often a range of about 10 pounds. If you feel that you may eventually work up to a bow pulling 70 pounds, concentrate on those models with a 60- to 70-pound adjustment, not 70 to 80 pounds. This allows you to start somewhere below the peak draw weight and condition yourself until you can draw the heavier poundage without strain.

Choosing a Handle Design

A bow that fits comfortably in your grip is extremely important. You'll likely shoot better with a bow that feels good in your grip than a bow that's uncomfortable in your hand. A large number of current models now feature replaceable rubber or wood grips, allowing you to find a size or shape that's compatible with your hand.

The shape of the handle, or riser, can affect the overall performance of the bow as well. Compound bow riser designs fall into one of three different categories; reflexed, straight or deflexed.

Models with a straight riser position the pockets where the limbs connect to the riser in a nearly straight line with the grip. Bows of the reflexed design position these pockets slightly ahead of the grip, while bows with deflexed limbs have the limb pockets noticeably rearward of the archer's hand position.

Bows with reflexed limbs feature the lowest brace height, generally measuring around 5 to 6 inches from the grip to the string (with the string not drawn). Straight bows generally have the string 7 or 8 inches to the rear of the grip, while deflexed bows can have a brace height of 10 inches. So what does all of this mean as far as performance is concerned?

Bows with lower brace heights are faster due to the fact that they have a longer power stroke. Bows with a reflexed riser design generally position the arrow rest closer to the string, which means the travel of the bowstring from full draw has more room to transfer the energy of the bow to the arrow. A bow with only a 5-inch brace height enjoys 5 more inches of power stroke than a bow with a 10-inch brace height. Bows of the deflexed design tend to be very forgiving when it comes to arrow flight and stability. The increased brace height positions the rest farther forward, giving arrows more room to straighten out from the moment the nock leaves the string and passes through or across the rest.

Mass/Weight

Oddly enough, a fully tricked-out bow that weighs 8 to 10 pounds is considered a heavy bow, and if

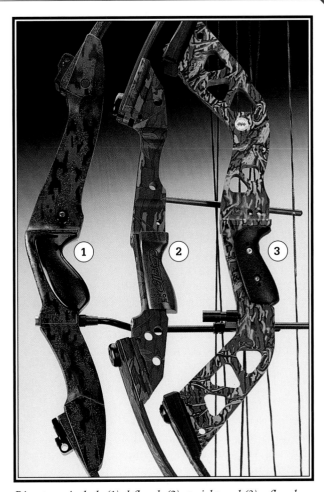

Riser types include (1) deflexed, (2) straight and (3) reflexed.

you have to carry one of that weight for very far, you'll be the first to agree. On the other hand, some of today's lighter models may weigh as little as 4 pounds, complete with sights, rest, quiver and four or five arrows.

Many shooters discover better, more consistent accuracy with a heavier bow that is easier to hold steady. And since most of us spend most of our time bowhunting whitetails sitting in a treestand, weight is usually not so much a factor. However, if you are ever faced with a long mile-or-two walk into a remote stand or find yourself using that bow on a western mule deer or elk hunt in the mountains, you may wish you had gone with a lighter model.

To reduce weight, bow manufacturers are now utilizing lightweight metals and even carbon to produce bows that are much nicer to pack. The risers now found on most bows today are made of either magnesium or aluminum. The most common are those made of magnesium, which is produced by pouring the molten metal into a die or mold. The process allows manufacturers to easily turn out practically identical risers quickly and economically. The one downside to a handle made in this manner is that on rare occasion, tiny air bubbles in the molten metal create small air pockets inside the casting, which can weaken the handle. And if a magnesium riser fails, it's usually at one of these spots.

Machined aluminum risers have gained in popularity with hunters who don't mind paying a little extra for a top-of-the-line model. Turned on a duplicating lathe with features and weight-reducing cutouts precisely milled, machined aluminum risers are more labor intensive, which will be reflected in the price of the bow. However, they are considered the strongest and most precise of all types of handle construction. Even so, they are not as light as die-cast magnesium handles. To help defray production costs, some bow makers are now utilizing forged aluminum risers that can be produced more economically. The process compresses the aluminum into a mold, giving the riser as much as 90 percent of its finished shape and features. Then it's finished out with a minimum amount of machining.

Carbon riser bows are just now finding their way into the bow market, and do offer a lot of promise. They are easier to produce than machined aluminum, and offer exceptional strength and preciseness. One thing is certain, those bows built with a carbon handle are light. In fact, some models weigh in at barely 3 pounds.

Accessories

Bowhunters have individual tastes and requirements, and the accessories found on one hunter's bow may be a full 180 from the accessory needs of another hunter. Accessories can range from very simple add-ons, such as a single-pin-type sight, to very sophisticated arrangements, such as an elevation self-adjusting pivoting multi-pin sighting system with fiber-optics, bubble level and maybe even lighted pins for shooting in the dim light of dawn and dusk.

When budgeting to purchase a new bow, the hunter should also factor in the cost of all the accessories required to make that bow "hunt ready." The list could include all or any combination of the following: bow sight, peep sight, arrow rest, stabilizer, overdraw, nocking loop, kisser button, wrist sling, string silencers, arrow holder and quiver. Other accessories, depending on taste, could include a new release, finger tab, shooting glove and maybe an arm guard. When a top-of-the-line bow is fully accessorized with only the

very best accessories, it is possible to invest as much in these as the bow itself. However, if the accessories you choose do contribute to better arrow placement, then never consider them expenses, but rather investments.

Hunting Arrows

Several factors come into play when determining the correct arrow for your bow. Many experienced bowhunters feel that proper arrow selection contributes as much to bowhunting success as the bow and accessories installed. So take the time to insure that you are shooting the proper arrow for your bow and draw length.

Aluminum arrows have all but replaced the wooden shafts dating from the late '50s and '60s. And we're now seeing the growing use of arrows made from extremely lightweight space-age graphite or carbon materials.

When selecting an arrow for your bow, concentrate on two main factors – the spine weight and length of the arrow. The spine weight of an arrow shaft basically refers to the stiffness of the shaft. This is largely determined by the diameter of the arrow and the thickness of the shaft walls. However, the spine of an arrow can also be affected by overall length as well.

An arrow that is too limber for the poundage of a bow will flex back and forth in flight, making it impossible to obtain optimum accuracy. This is usually most noticeable just as the arrow leaves the rest, but even a little wobble at launch can be enough to destroy downrange arrow placement.

On the other hand, an arrow that's too heavy for the poundage of a bow can really slow down arrow speed. Study the charts available at most archery dealers to determine the recommended shaft diameter and thickness for your draw length and the draw weight you are shooting. Aluminum arrow sizes are marked with a four-digit number which indicates the size of the shaft. The first two numbers refer to the diameter of the shaft in 1/64-inch increments, while the last two digits indicate the thickness of the shaft walls in thousands of an inch. For example, a 2117 shaft means that it is 21/64 inches in diameter and has a wall thickness of .017 inches.

The length of the arrow affects both its spine weight and overall weight. A shaft that is 2 inches longer than your determined draw length will display more whip than one that's cut perfectly for your draw. Plus the extra, unused 2 inches of shaft simply result in a heavier arrow.

In the past, carbon arrows were always very thin, slender shafts designated simply for the poundage bow a particular shaft happened to be spined. Most bowhunters despised the wimpy-looking shafts that required the use of a special rest for small-diameter arrows that developed a reputation for finicky flight and poor penetration on deer-sized game. Still, carbon arrows have won a growing following due to their strength, feather weights, speed and precision tolerances. And now a few carbon arrow makers are producing shafts which are more like the larger diameters of aluminum arrows, and these arrows continue to grow in popularity.

As bowhunting expert Dan Perez pointed out in the introduction to this chapter, carbon arrows are either straight or they're broken. There is no guessing.

Broadheads

It's hard to buy a "bad" broadhead these days. This isn't to say that some broadheads don't deliver less effective performance than others, but when compared to the broadheads that were available 25 years ago, most of today's hunting heads are far superior when it comes to good arrow flight, penetration or cutting.

The most popular designs among the current bowhunting crowd are the broadheads with replaceable blades. The best selling tend to be the three-bladed models with a cutting diameter of 1 1/8 to 1 1/4 inches, weighing 100 or 125 grains. Quality points of this design, such as the Muzzy or Thunderhead, are proven performers that fly straight and commonly pass completely through even big deer with a perfect broadside shot.

Whatever broadhead you choose, first make sure that it is compatible with the bow and arrow you shoot. Generally speaking, the heavier or larger the cutting diameter of the head, the larger the fletching it takes to properly control the arrow in flight. A heavier head contributes to overall arrow weight, resulting in slower arrow flight. And the wider the blade, the more it can be affected by planing. Also, oversized blades with an extremely wide cutting diameter may make contact with the shelf of the sight window when the arrow is pulled to full draw.

New and improved versions of the so-called mechanical broadheads continue to hit the market. These compactly fold the cutting blades forward into elongated slots in the ferrule of the point,

protecting the cutting edges while at the same time presenting an in-flight profile that is less affected by air currents. Most heads of this type rely on a small rubber "O" ring to keep the blades forward until impact with the target. Protruding shoulders at the end of each blade cause the cutting edges to be exposed as the blades fold rearward and the arrow continues on through the target.

The advantages of these heads include aerodynamics that allow broadheads of this design to fly nearly as true as a field point of the same weight, and the fact that the cutting edges are protected and remain sharp until shot into an animal. Some hunters have complained that points of this type often fail to open up, resulting in a lost deer. However, some of the newer designs have done much to eliminate this problem and are winning a strong following. For many veteran bowhunters, the jury is still out on the effectiveness of mechanical broadheads. However, those who do shoot them warn against using too light a bow, claiming that heavier-poundage bows help insure that the points open up properly upon impact.

Experienced bowhunters like Dan Perez spend a great deal of time tuning their arrows and broadheads to insure that they fly straight and true. An effort should be made to spin the arrow and broadhead on its tip to determine straightness. If you notice even a slight wobble where the broadhead meets the arrow insert, chances are it won't fly perfectly true. Many consistently successful bowhunters even take the time to insure that the cutting blades of the broadheads they shoot are in the exact same position on every arrow. Perez even numbers his broadhead-tipped arrows so he can make sure the ones in his quiver have been tested and fly true. The challenge of bowhunting whitetails is to get close enough to place an arrow exactly where it needs to go for a quick, clean kill. In other chapters of this book, well-known deer-hunting experts will take a look at the tactics, techniques and methods which can put an archer inside of 30 yards of big bucks. It's up to that hunter to be shooting the best equipment he or she can afford, and to have practiced enough with it to get the job done. 🦃

SECOND-CHANCE BUCK

by Dan Perez

Dan Perez with "Tall Tines," which scored 174 5/8 Boone & Crockett points

As I sat in the stand perched high in the giant old white oak, I reflected back on an encounter I had the previous season with a very tall-tined 10-pointer while hunting from the very same tree. That buck was sort of a legend in the area and was often referred to by local hunters as "Tall Tines."

Since I knew it would be a while before deer would begin to show, I let my mind drift back to the episode a year earlier. The memory of that buck was still crystal clear.

That afternoon, a cold northwest breeze had forced me to turn and face the old white oak, with my back to the wind. Just a short time later, I watched as old Tall Tines entered the field about 200 yards away. The buck fed into the bean field for a short distance, then moved on into the timber on my side of the field. Then I lost sight of him. I raised my M.A.D. 502 grunter to my lips and released four consecutive throaty tones, "eaa, eaa, eaa, eaa." No sooner had the last grunt sounded than I spotted the buck approaching from behind . . . and downwind.

At that point, my mind was racing almost as fast as my heart was pounding. Now Tall Tines was less than 12 yards away! But the jig was up. Like a statue, he stood behind the big old white oak and stared straight ahead. The tree was so huge, there was no way I could possibly reach around it and release an arrow. And even if I could, I was in no position to move a muscle.

The buck knew something wasn't right, and I knew it was only a matter of time before he would bolt. After what seemed like an eternity, that great whitetail whirled and ran back in the direction from which he came.

Sitting in that same stand again remembering last season's close encounter with such a magnificent buck sent chills up my spine. My thoughts were still on what I could have done differently when suddenly out of the corner of my eye I caught movement at the far end of the field. A very large-bodied buck with its neck stretched out and head low to the ground was tailing a couple of young yearling does. When I glassed him, I couldn't believe my eyes. It was Tall Tines.

It was too early in the rut for either of the two young does to be receptive to the buck's advances. On the chance that he would soon become bored with the yearlings, I slammed my rattling antlers together and worked them until he stopped and stared back in my direction. The buck's acknowledgement was my clue to stop rattling and put the antlers away.

At that point, all I could do was wait and hope the buck would soon abandoned the does and seek out the antler-clashing bucks. Sure enough, 30 minutes later he came right down the tree line, moving directly in my direction.

Old Tall Tines covered about 80 yards, then dropped down into a hollow and reappeared again on the opposite ridge a few minutes later. It was obvious that he was planning on circling downwind of my position. In order to maintain my composure, I kept repeating in my mind, "Any minute he's going to wind me." The big buck covered a lot of ground in a very short time.

He was about 10 steps from being directly downwind of my scent when he turned and headed in my direction once again.

Glimpses of hair moving through the vine-woven timber revealed that the buck was coming at a fast walk. I was at full draw before he hit the opening I had already chosen, and he was a quarter of the way across it when I vocally sounded a deep grunt. The buck came to a dead stop and looked in my direction. I steadied my 30-yard pin a few inches behind his right shoulder and unleashed the razor-sharp broadhead-tipped arrow.

My shot found its mark, and at the instant of impact the buck reacted by doing what I could best describe as a handstand flip. He swapped ends and slammed into a tree before crashing to the ground. Just as soon as the buck hit the ground, he was back on his feet. Then, like a bulldozer, he smashed his way through a vine-tangled web of brush before plowing into several trees. Once the deer was out of sight, I could still follow his direction by all of the snapping and popping of branches and limbs. Then all went silent.

I knew old Tall Tines was down for the count, but I sat quietly for about 15 minutes before going after him. When I hit the ground, I didn't even look for a blood trail. With the excitement that often accompanies anticipation, I stealthily stalked towards where I heard the last crash. Just 40 yards into that tangle of brush, I found my best buck ever sprawled in a shallow depression.

I let out a rebel yell I'm sure the coyotes on the next ridge are still talking about. When the realization that my pursuit of Tall Tines was over finally sunk in, I sat down on a log and relived the entire episode. In fact, I sat there with the old buck for over an hour before even thinking about moving him.

That great heavy-horned buck scored 174⅝ inches. Now, every time I look at the mount of this impressive whitetail my mind still reflects back to the first time I ever laid eyes upon him. I'll never forget the sight of the massive tall-tined buck as he stood out in the bean field, how the golden evening sun glistened off his antlers and how the buck's face was partially blurred by the puff of steam created when his breath left his nostrils and met the chilled November air.

The author with a big muzzleloader buck

The Other Deer Season –
Hunting with a Muzzleloader

by Toby Bridges

Since the 1960s, muzzleloading has gone through an accelerated metamorphosis, evolving from a nostalgic pastime into a true hunting sport. At one time muzzleloading shooters in North America were content just to master the art of loading and shooting the old-fashioned front-loading guns of the past. But today's muzzleloading shooter is a hunter with two goals in mind – to take full advantage of the special muzzleloader deer seasons now held in practically every state, and to shoot a rifle and load that will deliver the accuracy and knockdown power to get the job done.

The rifles preferred by the modern day "Jeremiah Johnson" are a far cry from the older designs dating from the late 1700s and early 1800s. Most original muzzleloading rifles, along with the modern reproductions of these guns, featured long barrels of 30 to 40 inches, and often weighed more than 10 pounds. A study of antique American longrifles, often referred to as Kentucky Rifles, would reveal that the average bore size was usually around .45 caliber. Correspondingly, the vast majority of new-made muzzleloading rifles offered during the 1960s and early 1970s also featured bores of this caliber.

My first muzzleloading "deer" rifle was one of the long-barreled .45-caliber percussion Dixie Gun Works "Squirrel Rifles." The Belgium-made frontloader shot extremely well with a 70-grain charge of FFFg black powder behind a tight cotton-cloth patched .440-inch diameter soft lead round ball. At 50 yards, the rifle and load would consistently print inside of 3 inches, which I considered pretty good for the rifle's traditional non-adjustable type open sights.

When I purchased that rifle back in 1964, there weren't many other models to choose from. And other than a couple of big .58-caliber Civil War rifled-musket reproductions then available, most all of the other sporting muzzleloaders on the market at the time were also offered in .45 caliber only. At age 14, I hunted with the rifle the first year I owned it, and I managed to take my first two muzzleloader whitetail bucks that fall. An Illinois buck shot at just 45 yards traveled nearly a quarter of a mile before going down, while a buck I shot in neighboring Missouri that season ran close to 200 yards before piling up.

Today, I wouldn't even consider going after whitetails with a .45-caliber rifle loaded with a patched round ball, even if I could get it to shoot accurately with powder charges of 100 or more grains of black powder or Pyrodex. The load used to take my first two muzzleloader-harvested whitetails put the light 128-grain .440-inch round ball out of the muzzle at just 1,800 or so f.p.s., which means the tiny sphere of soft lead was good for only 920 foot-pounds of energy at the muzzle. And even if I could up the powder charge another 20 grains and get the ball moving out of the bore at 2,000 f.p.s., it would still only have around 1,135 foot-pounds of muzzle energy.

Early in the 1970s, the .50-caliber rifles quickly replaced the pipsqueak .45 as the most popular caliber. This change was due to the fact that more and more "muzzleloader only" seasons were being established and an ever growing number of whitetail hunters were turning to muzzleloaders in order to enjoy this "third season" opportunity.

Many experienced muzzleloading hunters consider the .50-caliber bore the optimum bore size for a muzzleloading big-game rifle. It can be stoked up to deliver considerably greater punch than is possible with the smaller .45-caliber rifles. And for a .54-caliber muzzleloader to deliver more knockdown power than the .50 caliber requires a greater investment in powder and bullet weight. Even then, the return is generally not much more than greater recoil.

The .490-inch to .495-inch round balls commonly fired out of a .50-caliber rifle weigh between 178 and 180 grains. Charged with 100 grains of FFg black powder or the volume equivalent of Pyrodex "RS" or "Select," the load will get the ball out of the muzzle at between 1,800 and 1,900 f.p.s., depending some on barrel length. The energy produced will be between 1,300 and 1,400 foot-pounds.

Personally, I feel that the traditional patched round ball is the absolute worst projectile the muzzleloading hunter can use on whitetails, or any other big-game animal for that matter. Out to about 50 or 75 yards, the .50- or .54-caliber rifles loaded with a hefty powder charge and a patched ball generally produce ample punch to cleanly down even a good buck, but once the range extends out to 100 yards or maybe a little farther, the round ball looses just too much "oomph" to consistently take deer-sized game. A .50-caliber rifle that produces 1,800 f.p.s. at the muzzle with a 178-grain .490-inch round ball is good for only about 600 foot-pounds of energy out at 100 yards – hardly enough to be reliable on a big buck that could weigh between 200 and 300 pounds.

Serious muzzleloading whitetail hunters have really turned away from the patched soft lead round ball. Those hunters who favor a traditionally styled rifle now tend to opt for those models that feature a slightly faster rate of rifling twist for acceptable accuracy with longer and heavier conical bullets or maxi-style bullets. Favorite designs include the Thompson/Center Arms "Maxi-Hunter," the Buffalo Bullet Company "Maxi-Bullet" and the Hornady "Great Plains Bullet." Most of these designs more than double the weight of the round ball for a particular caliber, and with a stout powder charge of 90 to 110 grains (FFg black powder or Pyrodex RS/Select) can really turn a muzzleloader into a real whitetail stopper.

Being so much heavier than the round ball for the same caliber rifle, these great hunks of lead are slower at the muzzle. A 100-grain charge of FFg black powder will push a 385-grain Hornady Great Plains Bullet from a 28-inch barreled .50-caliber Thompson/Center Hawken at about 1,500 f.p.s. However, due to the added weight of the heavy conical bullet, this translates into 1,925 foot-pounds of muzzle energy. And being more aerodynamic than the patched round ball, this big bullet retains velocity and downrange energy much better. At 100 yards, this load would still hit a whitetail buck with around 1,300 foot-pounds of punch – more than twice the knockdown power produced by the same powder charge and round ball at that distance.

I was the first bowhunter in my hometown to own a compound bow, and likewise was one of the very first muzzleloader hunters in my home state of Illinois to make the switch to a modern in-line percussion ignition rifle. My first in-line rifle was a .50-caliber Knight MK-85, Serial No. 31.

This very modernistic muzzleloader changed muzzleloading forever. While not the first rifle of in-line type percussion ignition, the Knight MK-85 was the first to bring to the modern-day muzzleloading hunter a frontloading big-game rifle that was loaded with user-friendly and performance-minded features. These included modern rifle lines and balance, a center-mounted nipple for straight-in fire from the percussion cap, a receiver that came drilled and tapped for easy scope mounting, a modern side safety (plus a secondary screw-in safety), a removable breech plug for easy and thorough cleaning of the bore, and a short and fast handling 24-inch barrel. The barrel's fast one-turn-in-28-inches rate of rifling twist provided exceptional accuracy with an equally modern projectile system that relied on a small plastic sabot to transfer the spin of the rifling to a modern jacketed handgun bullet.

It has been the combination of refined in-line ignition rifles and polymer saboted jacketed or all-copper bullets that has brought muzzleloader performance to new, never-before-reached effectiveness. With two of the new 50-grain Pyrodex Pellets behind a saboted 250-grain .45-caliber jacketed hollow-point, a 24-inch barreled .50-caliber in-line ignition muzzleloader is capable of producing a muzzle velocity of around 1,650 f.p.s. with right at 1,500 foot-pounds of muzzle energy. Out at 100 yards, the bullet still hits a whitetail with around 1,200 foot-pounds of knockdown power.

During the mid 1990s several muzzleloader manufacturers introduced new models that eliminated the old-style percussion cap for providing the fire for ignition.

These new in-line rifles instead relied on much hotter No. 209 shotshell primers that easily put 10 to 15 times the fire into the powder charge. The added spark has not only made models like the Knight D.I.S.C. Rifle and Thompson/Center Arms Encore 209x50 Magnum more sure-fire, even in bad weather, but they also more completely burn heavier magnum charges of powder. Both Knight and Thompson/Center have heavily promoted the use of three 50-grain Pyrodex Pellets (150-grain powder charge) behind a saboted bullet of 180 to 300 grains. With some of the lighter bullets, these two muzzleloading rifle makers are claiming velocities in excess of 2,000 f.p.s.

Thompson/Center Arms claim that their Encore 209x50 Magnum is "the world's most powerful .50-caliber muzzleloader." Shooting a three 50-grain Pyrodex Pellet load behind a saboted 240-grain jacketed hollow-point bullet out of the 26-inch barreled break-open in-line ignition muzzleloader,

The Savage Model 10ML II .50-caliber muzzleloader

factory supplied ballistics claim muzzle velocities of 2,203 f.p.s. This calculates into 2,580 foot-pounds of energy at the muzzle. Out at 100 yards, the bullet will drive home with around 1,600 foot-pounds of knockdown power. And all the way out at 200 yards, the 240-grain jacketed hollow point would still cleanly bring down a big whitetail buck with more than 1,000 foot-pounds of remaining energy.

As hot as this rifle and load may seem, there is now a new king when it comes to high-performance muzzleloaders. The Savage Model 10ML II is currently the only .50-caliber muzzleloader that is fully capable of pushing a saboted bullet out of the muzzle at velocities greater than 2,300 f.p.s., and to do so it does not rely on hefty loads of Pyrodex or Pyrodex Pellets. Instead, this controversial new frontloader relies on hotter and cleaner-burning modern smokeless powders, such as IMR-4227, Vihtavouri N110 or Accurate Arms XMP5744.

With a 44-grain charge of Vihtavouri N110 behind a saboted .452-inch 250-grain Hornady XTP, the new Savage Model 10ML II launches the jacketed hollow point out of the 24-inch barrel at around 2,350 f.p.s. for an astounding 3,065 foot-pounds of whitetail-taking wallop. The same powder charge behind a heavier 300-grain XTP is still good for around 2,275 f.p.s. and more than 3,400 foot-pounds of energy.

I have hunted with every rifle and load detailed here, and as this was written, I have harvested more than 200 whitetails with muzzleloading rifles, including several dozen bucks that qualify for the muzzleloading record books. As much as I still enjoy shooting the old-fashioned muzzleloading guns from the past, I leave nostalgia hanging on the gun rack at home whenever I'm headed out to hunt a good buck. Now and then I may rely on a favorite old "round-ball rifle" from the past to fill a few bonus doe tags, but when I'm out to hang my tag on a dandy buck you can bet that I'll be packing as modern and as efficient a rifle and load as the law will allow.

Selecting a Muzzleloading Deer Rifle

Muzzleloader hunting has become more performance driven than at any time in history. Generally speaking, today's muzzleloading hunter wants to be packing the most efficient, accurate and hardest-hitting hunting rifle regulations permit. And a great selection of very modern in-line ignition rifles meets the needs of even the most performance minded of hunters.

Still, for a declining number of muzzleloader fans, hunting with old-fashioned muzzleloaders of traditional design offers a portal through which they can step back in time and experience what it was like to hunt with muzzleloaded firearms from the past. Fortunately, in most states the current muzzleloader hunting regulations fulfill the wishes of nearly every hunter who wants to head for the deer woods with his or her favorite muzzleloader thrown over their shoulder, no matter how modern or how traditional its design.

Before deciding on a particular style or design of a rifle, a hunter should first determine the style or type of projectile to be shot. It takes an entirely different rate of rifling twist to get optimum accuracy from either the patched round ball or a conical bullet.

Accuracy with a patched round ball is based on a paradox – a projectile that is spun by rifling that the ball never touches. The tightly woven cotton cloth patch that grips the ball fulfills several roles. First, the material must be of sufficient thickness to make up the difference between the slightly smaller ball diameter and the actual land-to-land measurement of the bore. Upon loading, the cloth should ideally be compressed somewhat for a tight fit around the ball and into the grooves of the rifling for a proper gas seal when the powder ignites.

As the ball is pushed down the bore by the burning

powder charge, the tight fit of the patch into the grooves transfers the spin of the rifling to the ball. Centuries of shooting the patched round ball out of muzzleloaded rifles have determined that the ideal rate of rifling twist for best performance with the spheres of soft lead are grooves that spin with a relatively slow rate of one turn in 60 to 72 inches. Rifling that spins with a much faster rate of twist generally produces poor or mediocre accuracy with the patched round ball. This is especially true when shooting hefty hunting charges in either a .50-or .54-caliber deer rifle that can cause the patch and ball to travel down the bore so fast that the combination resists being spun by the rifling. Old timers referred to the condition as stripping the rifling.

Conical muzzleloading projectiles come in a variety of styles, lengths and weights. One of the first truly successful conical bullets that found a strong following with today's muzzleloader deer hunter was the Thompson/Center "Maxi-Ball." Firearms designer Warren Center came up with the bullet design and built his popular Thompson/Center Arms "Hawken" rifle around it back in 1970. For the 20 years that followed, the rifle and heavy lead elongated bullet became the number-one choice of muzzleloading hunters. Following in the footsteps of that bullet have been several other successful conical muzzleloaded hunting projectiles, including the Buffalo Bullet Company "Maxi-Bullet" and the Hornady "Great Plains Bullet."

While the designs may vary slightly from bullet to bullet, the majority share a common trait. Most conical bullets are nearly twice as long as their diameter, and weigh twice or more the weight of a round ball for the same caliber rifle. Being so much longer, elongated muzzleloading projectiles require a faster rate of rifling twist for proper stabilization in flight. A long, heavy bullet that is not properly spun on its axis will not shoot accurately.

When Thompson/Center Arms introduced its Hawken rifle, the company elected to rifle the bore of the 28-inch barrel with a one-turn-in-48-inches rate of twist. At best this rate of twist is a compromise – with moderate powder charges it will often shoot well with a patched round ball while still delivering a heavier conical with enough accuracy for hunting. However, today's hunter isn't content to hunt with a rifle that's a compromise and the modern in-line rifles with faster rates of twist have become favored by hunters who prefer the added knockdown power of longer, heavier conical bullets. Most of these rifles feature rifling with a much faster one-turn-in-20-to-32 inches rate of twist. Out of a quality muzzleloading rifle with a quality barrel, some of these bullets are quite

capable of printing tight hundred-yard groups.

Muzzleloader hunting loads made up around a small plastic sabot, or cup, containing a modern jacketed or all-copper bullet have now all but replaced the big heavy lead conical bullets. Estimations from knowledgeable muzzleloading authorities suggest that as many as 75 percent of all muzzleloader hunters today rely on saboted bullets when hunting deer and other big game.

Several different variations of sabots have been introduced to the market since the mid-1980s, but one particular style has stood out as the most popular – and as the most accurate. Muzzleload Magnum Products, a small plastic injection molding company located near Harrison, Arkansas, can be credited with popularizing this system. And while the simple "shotgun wad" styling of the sabot they produce today may not look all that much different than the sabots the company produced a decade or two ago, today's sabots incorporate better design in the geometry of the base, which must contain the pressure of the burning powder charge. Plus Muzzleload Magnum Products is now using much tougher and more resilient polymers to produce a stronger, superior sabot.

Generally speaking, there are several different sizes available for each suitable big-game caliber. For the popular .50-caliber, Muzzleload Magnum Products offers two sabots. One is for loading and shooting .429-inch diameter bullets, such as those for the .44 Magnum handguns, the other is for loading and shooting .451-inch to .452-inch diameter bullets, such as those loaded into .45 Long Colt or .454 Casull handgun ammunition, plus a few new all-copper bullets designed specifically for muzzleloading big-game rifles. The concept allows the hunter to load and shoot a better performing bullet than a simple hunk of soft lead.

Like conical "maxi-style" bullets, saboted bullets require a fast rate of twist for best stabilization and

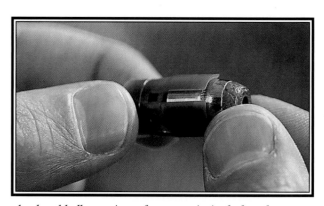

A saboted bullet requires a fast rate twist in the barrel.

accuracy. The majority of today's in-line ignition rifles come with a one-turn-in-24-to-28 inches rifling twist, and that's the window that seems to shoot saboted bullets best. Experienced .50-caliber sabot-shooting hunters have come to realize that out of most rifles, a saboted .452-inch diameter bullet will outshoot a saboted .429-inch diameter bullet. The widely accepted explanation is that the slightly larger diameter .45 bullet requires a sabot with thinner petals that are more pliable and peel away from the bullet quicker once the combination leaves the muzzle. This quicker sabot has less time to affect bullet flight.

For hunters using their favorite .50-caliber muzzleloading rifle, the choice of bullet weight is broad, from as light as 180 grains all the way up to more than 325 grains. For use on whitetail deer, saboted bullets of 240 to 300 grains tend to be the most popular. These develop impressive energy levels when shot with hefty powder charges, produce considerably lighter recoil than the heavy "maxi" bullets, and retain whitetail-stopping energy well out past 100 yards.

Use the Right Propellant

For more than 650 years muzzleloading shooters around the world could use only one propellant – black powder. However, since the mid-1970s, several new black-powder substitutes have been introduced, and these new powders have made today's muzzleloaders better performing, cleaner to shoot, and harder hitting.

During the more than six centuries that black powder remained the only muzzleloader propellant, the make-up of the powder remained basically unchanged – various combinations of saltpeter, ground charcoal and sulfur. The resulting explosive has propelled untold billions of rounds down the barrels of frontloading guns through the ages.

The fact that black powder is classified as a "Class A Explosive" has made this traditional muzzleloader propellant harder and harder to obtain. Strict local, state and federal regulations govern its manufacture, transportation, storage and sale. For many muzzleloading gun dealers and other outdoor retailers, black powder has become too big of a hassle to sell.

Still for some rifles, especially many of the older traditionally styled muzzleloaders, black powder continues to perform better than any of the modern-day substitutes. Few competition shooters will load anything but black powder behind the patched round balls required in most official National Muzzle Loading Rifle Association sanctioned

matches, while many of the heavy conical bullets which are unable to actually compact the powder charge will only produce consistent performance with easily ignited black powder. Rifles of .50 and .54 caliber should be loaded with black powder of FFg granulation, while many shooters use finer and faster burning FFFg in muzzleloaders .45 caliber and smaller. This propellant, which is older than muzzleloading itself, leaves a great deal of fouling in the bore with each shot, and for best accuracy the shooter or hunter should take time to wipe this fouling from the rifling before loading the next shot.

The substitute Pyrodex was first introduced by a small Washington-state-based company during the mid-1970s and was put into commercial production by Hodgdon Powder Company later that decade. Until recently, it remained the only successful substitute for black powder guns.

While the company offers Pyrodex in a number of granulations, of most importance to the muzzleloading deer hunter will be "RS" (Rifle/Shotgun) and "Select," which is a premium grade of "RS." These two powders can be loaded on a volume equivalent with FFg black powder. (Note: By actual weight, Pyrodex is approximately 20 percent lighter than black powder, but when measured with the same volumetric measurers used to determine black powder loads, the substitute will deliver approximately the same velocities as the same volume of FFg black powder.)

To get higher velocities and greater energy levels with saboted bullets, many muzzleloading deer hunters are loading and shooting finer "P" (Pistol) grade Pyrodex. This is the equivalent of FFFg black powder and when loaded in the same volumes as "RS" or "Select" will generally give about a 10 percent higher velocity.

Loose-grained Pyrodex has a reputation for being slightly harder to ignite than black powder, and has been recommended for use only in percussion ignition rifles. And even in some percussion ignition rifles the shooter must use one of the hotter percussion caps, winged musket caps or primer ignition systems to insure that the muzzleloader fires when the trigger is pulled. Compacting the loose-grained Pyrodex slightly with 30 to 40 pounds of pressure on the ramrod when the projectile is seated also helps insure ignition. Just be sure to use the same amount of ramrod pressure for each shot or accuracy could vary.

Loading the hotter ignition in-line percussion rifles became a lot quicker and easier during the late 1990s with the introduction of Pyrodex Pellets. Hodgdon Powder Company now offers these in several different charge weights, allowing the shooter to drop in any given combination of pellets to develop a favorite charge for a particular in-line rifle. For instance, three 30-grain pellets equal a 90-grain charge, two 50-grain pellets make up a 100-grain charge, and so forth. And "dropping in" is all that charging requires. The pellets are removed from the container and simply dropped into the bore. Then the projectile is seated directly over the powder. Care should be taken to not crush the pellets when seating the bullet.

One end of each pellet is lightly coated with a more sensitive igniter, and this should be inserted toward the source of the flame for ignition. The pellets also feature a tiny hole running lengthwise through the center. This allows the flame from the ignition to travel through the middle of the pellet as well as along all sides to ensure a complete burn. Many shooters have turned to in-line rifle models with primer ignition to guarantee that the pellets will be ignited and burnt.

The hotter flame produced by big primers like the No. 209 shotshell primer also ensures a more complete burn of magnum pellet powder charges. A number of in-line ignition rifle manufacturers are now promoting the use of three 50-grain Pyrodex Pellets (150-grain powder charge) behind saboted bullets for maximum performance from these rifles. Out of many modern in-line rifles, muzzle velocities now exceed 2,000 f.p.s.

Two other more recent black powder substitutes are CLEAR SHOT, now produced by black powder maker GOEX, and Clean Shot, from Clean Shot Technologies. Both are available in loose-grain form, while Clean Shot is offered in 30- and 50-grain pellets as well. Some tests have shown the Clean Shot pellets to produce nearly 10% higher velocities than the same powder charge made up with Pyrodex Pellets.

Until recently, shooting modern nitrocellulose based smokeless powders in muzzleloaders had been strictly taboo. But with the introduction of the Savage Model 10ML II a couple of years ago, all that has changed. And so has muzzleloading.

Here is a frontloading big-game rifle that can be loaded with all of the traditional muzzleloading propellants already covered, plus powders which until now had been reserved only for modern big-bore handguns and centerfire rifles. These powders include IMR-4227, Accurate Arms XMP5744 and Vihtavouri N110. Powder charges of around 45 grains behind a saboted 250-grain jacketed .452-inch diameter bullet produce muzzle velocities of around 2,200 to 2,300 f.p.s. and energy levels of

around 3,000 foot-pounds. And in addition to the improved ballistics, this rifle is more economical to load, and has nearly maintenance free loads (thanks to non-corrosive smokeless powders), and the considerably softer recoil of these loads make this rifle more enjoyable to shoot.

NOTE: DO NOT load and shoot modern smokeless powders in any muzzleloader designed and built to shoot "black powder or Pyrodex only!" The Savage Model 10ML is the only muzzleloader engineered to handle the pressures of smokeless powders.

Accessories

Muzzleloading is a sport in which the participant can outfit himself or herself with every imaginable accessory available, or succeed by using only a handful of necessities. The degree to which a muzzleloading shooter accessorizes a frontloading deer rifle is entirely a personal one.

Keep in mind that the more gear you carry into the deer woods, the more things you have to keep organized. Hunters of centuries past often carried powder horns, powder flasks, patching, a ball or bullet bag, a short or ball starter, a powder measure, a patch knife, a capper or pan primer, a nipple or vent pick, a cleaning jag, maybe a bullet puller, and possibly a few tools in a leather bag they toted on their side. Today's hunter has learned to keep things simple.

Instead of heading out into the wilderness for weeks on end, most of us look at a day in the deer woods as just that – a day in the deer woods. And to be ready for all the action that day may hold in store, the weight- and space-conscious muzzleloading hunter now carries just enough loading components for five or six shots. The powder charges are commonly pre-measured at home or at camp, then carried in small plastic tubes known as speed loaders that often also include a compartment for holding a single projectile or a bullet and sabot. With a half-dozen of these, a capper filled with percussion caps or a small zip-lock plastic bag with a supply of primers, plus a cleaning jag and a dozen or so cotton cleaning patches stuffed into a jacket pocket, most hunters are more than equipped for a day of muzzleloader deer hunting.

It's always smart to pack enough loading components to get the job done. However, the hunter who has chosen his rifle wisely, has matched it with the proper powder and projectile, shoots it enough to know its outermost effective range, and can properly place shots should find that the first shot is the only shot needed. 🦃

NEW LIFE FOR THE .45 CALIBER?

by Toby Bridges

Less than a half-century ago, back before whitetail populations began to expand into all suitable habitat, 20th-Century muzzle-loading marksmen honed their shooting skills at formal and informal shooting matches held on a regular basis all across the country. Paper targets, or even swinging steel silhouettes for that matter, didn't require a big-bore muzzleloader to score a hit, and frontloading rifles of .45 caliber were popular with the then growing crowd of black powder burners. A quality rifle in that caliber was usually deadly accurate, and the .45s were reasonably economical to shoot, requiring only moderate powder charges and lightweight 128- to 130-grain patched round balls to produce target-quality performance.

By the end of the 1970s, most states where the whitetail is found had established special "muzzleloader-only" or "primitive-weapons" deer-hunting seasons. As muzzleloading shooters began aligning their sights on deer-sized game rather than paper or steel targets, they quickly realized that it took a slightly larger bore size to effectively bring down whitetail deer, especially a big, mature buck. In just a few short years, .50 caliber rifles became the number-one choice of the modern-day muzzleloading hunter. Rifles of this caliber now make up nearly 90 percent of all muzzleloaders sold annually.

In recent years, several in-line ignition muzzle-loading rifle manufacturers have worked hard to revive interest in the .45-caliber bore size. However, instead of promoting the use of light patched round balls, these gun makers are now pushing the use of saboted .40-caliber/10mm handgun bullets of 150 to 200 grains. And instead of moderate 60- or 70-grain charges of FFFg black powder, they're getting much better velocities and energy levels by stoking these rifles up with three 50-grain Pyrodex Pellets (150-grain powder charge). In fact, one maker claims that with one of the magnum powder charges their 26-inch barreled, No. 209 shotshell primer-ignited .45 rifle is capable of getting a saboted 150-grain bullet out of the muzzle at more than 2,600 f.p.s.!

At the muzzle, this load develops right at 2,250 foot-pounds of energy. However, because the .40-caliber/10mm bullet is so light, velocity and energy drop off really quickly. At 100 yards, a 150-grain jacketed or all-copper bullet is still moving along at around 1,950 f.p.s., with around 1,260 foot-pounds of energy. However, by the time that tiny bullet reaches 200 yards, it has slowed to around 1,400 f.p.s. and retains only 650 foot-pounds of knockdown energy. While this is hardly enough to consistently get the job done, the .45-caliber rifle's maker is still promoting it as a 200-yard deer rifle.

For my whitetail hunting, I'll stick with a .50-caliber loaded with a saboted 250-grain or heavier bullet. With a three 50-grain Pyrodex Pellet load, most .50-caliber rifles loaded with a 250-grain projectile will deliver it with more than 900 foot-pounds of energy out at 200 yards. The new Savage Model 10ML II loaded with a smokeless powder load to get muzzle velocity up over 2,300 f.p.s. will hammer a 250-grain bullet home with 1,200 foot-pounds of energy out at 200 yards – that's nearly twice the knockdown power of the pipsqueak .45 and saboted .40-caliber bullets at that distance.

A perfectly mushroomed all-copper .50-caliber saboted bullet

This hunter used a Thompson Contender to harvest this 162-inch B&C whitetail.

Hunting Whitetails
with a One-Hand Gun

with Larry Weishuhn

The present abundance of whitetail deer provides us with some of the longest hunting seasons we have ever known. In many areas around the country, whitetail populations have become overabundant, and some states now allow the die-hard hunter to stay in the deer woods for 3 to 4 months each fall. To take full advantage of this lengthy season often means having to hunt with bow . . . muzzleloader . . . and modern firearms. And it has been these expanded hunting opportunities that have resulted in the growing number of hunters now picking up archery and muzzleloading gear for the very first time.

Many hunting industry experts feel that the same thing could happen with handgunning if more states established separate handgun seasons for deer.

Opponents claim that with the long and liberal modern gun season we currently enjoy, the present day pistolero has more than ample opportunity to take a whitetail or two with a favored handgun. And many are doing just that. Even with the limited opportunities, there is now a slowly growing number of deer hunters who are leaving their centerfire rifles or slug-shooting shotguns at home to carry a hard-hitting big-game handgun into the field, if for no other reason than for the challenge of taking a good buck with a one-hand gun.

One of those pistol-packing whitetail hunters is none other than respected whitetail hunting authority and professional wildlife biologist Larry Weishuhn. And when carrying one of today's deadly accurate handguns designed specifically for the hunter, this very knowledgeable whitetail hunter says there is absolutely no reason to feel under-gunned.

"Probably the first truly serious big-game hunting handgun available at an affordable price to the average hunter was the single-shot Contender from Thompson/Center Arms," states Weishuhn.

This break-open single-shot handgun has been around since the early 1970s and through the years has been offered in a variety of calibers and barrel lengths. The 10-inch and 14-inch barrels, which can be easily interchanged onto the same frame, have been the most popular. Weishuhn points out that one of the most popular size chambers for hunting deer-sized game in the past has been the old venerable .30/30 Winchester cartridge.

While the .30/30 cartridge, with factory loads available for the millions of lever-action Winchester and Marlin rifles chambered for the cartridge, is not considered as much of a whitetail cartridge by today's rifle deer hunter, properly handloaded it becomes a good 100-yard whitetail round for the Contender pistol. With most 150-grain round-nose factory ammunition, a 14-inch Contender barrel is good for right at 2,125 f.p.s. at the muzzle, generating close to 1,500 foot-pounds of muzzle energy. Out at 100 yards, the bullet would still hit with more than 1,000 foot-pounds of knockdown power. Carefully crafted custom handloads, utilizing spire-point type bullets, improve the performance of the .30/30 cartridge out of this and other handguns chambered for it.

(NOTE: Do not load spire-point bullets into any .30/30 cartridge intended for use in a lever-action rifle with a tubular magazine. Due to recoil, the sharp point of one cartridge riding on the primer of the cartridge ahead of it could cause detonation.)

Larry Weishuhn has hunted extensively with the T/C Contender in a variety of calibers, plus a wide range of other single-shot designs, a few revolvers and even several semi-auto handguns. To him, the "type" of handgun isn't as important as the game-taking effectiveness of the caliber chosen, or the gun's and shooter's ability to place hits exactly where they need to go.

"Of all the handguns I have hunted deer and other big game with, easily my favorite has been the Thompson/Center Arms 15-inch-barreled single-shot Encore in .30/06 Springfield caliber. It's the handgun I currently hunt with," says Weishuhn.

His favorite load for the handgun is available as a commercial load from Federal Cartridge Company and comes with a 165-grain Nosler Ballistic Tip bullet. Larry has a 2.5-7x T/C handgun scope mounted on the barrel sighted to hit 1.5 inches high at 100 yards, where the handgun can keep most hits within a 1-inch group. He has great confidence in the big single-shot handgun rig and has used it to take a variety of big game, including moose, elk, caribou, bear, mule deer and prong-horns, as well as several dandy whitetails. His best taken with the .30/06 Encore was a beautiful buck that gross scored 173 Boone and Crockett points.

For Whitetails, Shoot Enough Handgun

Watch enough old cowboy movies and you would begin to believe that the meanest and hardest hitting handgun ever introduced was the old Colt single-action Army revolver, often referred to as the "Peacemaker." Bad guys just didn't have a chance once the good guy had been forced to draw his trusty Colt six-shooter. And when our hero began to blaze away, nothing was too big or too far away for the handgun. But that was in the movies.

In real life, the Colt single-action .44- and .45-caliber revolvers were less than effective for bad guys or for putting meat on the table. This historical handgun, which was first introduced in 1872, has been chambered through the years for dozens of different calibers, but easily the two most favored have been the .44/40 Winchester and the .45 Long Colt. Commercially loaded ammunition is still readily available for both cartridges, and as popular as they were during the late 1800s, neither caliber delivers enough knockdown power for consistently taking game much bigger than a sizeable coyote. Whitetail hunting cartridges they're not, but they can still be legally used to hunt deer in many states.

Keep in mind that until the 1890s, cartridges were loaded with black powder, and with hundreds of thousands of old guns still out there being shot, ammunition makers continue to load low-pressure (and low-velocity) loads to insure the safety of the shooter.

Winchester-Olin's current Super-X load for the .44/40 cartridge puts a 200-grain soft-point bullet out of a 22-inch "rifle" barrel at 1,190 f.p.s., developing just 629 foot-pounds of muzzle energy. At 100 yards, the bullet hits with less than 450 foot-pounds of remaining energy. Out of a 6- or 7½-inch handgun barrel, the ballistics are even less impressive. Federal Cartridge's factory load for .45 Long Colt handguns puts a 225-grain semi-wadcutter out of a 6-inch revolver barrel at around 900 f.p.s., which translates into only 405 foot-pounds of energy. At just 50 yards, this has diminished to about 370 foot-pounds of remaining knockdown power. These are hardly the ballistics of efficient whitetail cartridges.

.357 Magnum

One of the most over-rated handgun cartridges today is the .357 Magnum. This "souped-up" version of the .38 Special, introduced by Smith & Wesson for their heavy-frame revolver in 1935, was considered the "most powerful handgun cartridge in the world" for some 20 years, until the introduction of the .44 Remington Magnum in 1955. As far as energy levels are concerned, the hardest-hitting load for the .357 Magnum offered by Federal Cartridge Company puts a 125-grain Hi-Shock jacketed hollow-point out of a 6-inch barrel at 1,458 f.p.s., with a not-so-whopping 580 foot-pounds of energy. At 50 yards, the bullet has only 430 foot-pounds of energy remaining. That's hardly enough to consistently bring down a whitetail buck pushing 300 pounds on the hoof. But here again we have a cartridge that is still allowed for use on deer-sized game in many states.

.44 Remington Magnum

The .44 Magnum continues to be one of the more powerful revolver cartridges available today. Developed jointly by Smith & Wesson and Remington as a harder-hitting replacement for the .357 Magnum, the cartridge has been one of the most widely used by handgun deer hunters. This is primarily due to the fact that many states will not permit the use of "bottle-neck" centerfire rifle cartridges in a handgun for hunting whitetails.

Factory ballistics for the .44 Magnum put a jacketed 240-grain bullet out of a 6-inch barrel at around 1,180 f.p.s. At this velocity the bullet would develop close to 750 foot-pounds of muzzle energy. Out at 50 yards, the bullet would hit a whitetail with around 625 foot-pounds of energy. With a good hit, it would still bring down a big buck, but once the range extends out to 100 yards that 240-grain jacketed hollow point would be just barely breaking 1,000 f.p.s., hitting with about 550 foot-pounds of punch. At that range the much-touted .44 Magnum begins to get a little iffy when it comes to performance on deer-sized game.

.454 Casull

Deer hunters who prefer the revolver design may want to take a closer look at those models chambered for the .454 Casull cartridge. This is a real powerhouse that with some ammunition delivers more energy at 100 yards than the .44 Remington Magnum develops at the muzzle!

Out of a 10-inch-barreled Freedom Arms Model 454 revolver, Winchester's Partition Gold ammunition loaded with a 260-grain jacketed hollow-point bullet produces a muzzle velocity of just over 1,800 f.p.s., which develops into some 1,880 foot-pounds of energy. And when this bullet reaches the 100-yard mark, it still drives home with more than 1,300 foot-pounds of whitetail-taking energy.

In their zest to control the length of shots taken at deer by handgun hunters, many state game departments have inadvertently forced hunters to go afield with handguns that are less than adequate to get the job done cleanly. Handguns chambered for cartridges like the .44/40 Winchester, .45 Long Colt or .357 Magnum are much better suited for punching holes in targets or varmints than game as large as a whitetail buck.

Centerfire Rifle Cartridges

Where legal, handgun hunters are moving away from these so-called "handgun cartridges" and turning to big break-open single-shot or bolt-action pistols chambered for popular centerfire rifle cartridges. The .30/06 T/C Encore preferred by whitetail hunting expert Larry Weishuhn at the beginning of this chapter is the kind of serious hunting handgun that continues to grow in popularity. Take a look at the following ballistics and you'll see why.

Since introducing their Contender single-shot break-open handgun design back in the 1960s, Thompson/Center Arms has replaced many of the early size chambers with some new choices, most of which are better known as "high-powered" rifle cartridges. At one time, the company offered more than two dozen interchangeable barrels for this handgun in calibers ranging from .22 Long Rifle to .45/70 Government. With a half-dozen different barrels, shooters could own one extremely versatile single-shot handgun.

.30/30 Winchester

Factory-loaded ammunition in .30/30 Winchester continues to be among the five best-selling rifle cartridges sold today. This isn't because it is such a great deer-hunting caliber, but because since its introduction in 1895, an estimated 10 million rifles have been sold in that caliber. Most of these have been lever-action designs, including the Winchester Model 94, Marlin Model 336 and

Savage Model 99. (Note: The .30/30 Winchester holds the distinction of being the first American small-bore smokeless powder sporting cartridge.)

At best, out of a 22- to 24-inch-barreled rifle, factory-loaded ammunition with 150- or 170-grain round-nosed bullets should be considered a "short-range" deer cartridge. From a 14-inch handgun barrel, 150-grain factory loads will produce a muzzle velocity of around 2,100 f.p.s., with around 1,470 foot-pounds of energy. At 100 yards, the bullet has slowed to around 1,875 f.p.s. and hits with right at 1,200 foot-pounds of energy. It's still a good performer on whitetails.

The single-shot design of handguns like the T/C Contender permit the .30/30 Winchester cartridge to be handloaded with more aerodynamically shaped spire-point bullets with a higher ballistic coefficient for superior downrange performance. Several different powders allow bullets like the 150-grain Nosler Ballistic Tip to be handloaded to velocities of around 2,200 f.p.s. from a 14-inch barrel. This gives a muzzle energy of around 1,600 foot-pounds and a 100-yard muzzle energy of close to 1,350 foot-pounds. At 200 yards, this bullet would still hit with more than 1,100 foot-pounds of stopping power.

.35 Remington

Here is another popular lever-action rifle cartridge with outstanding application as a hunting handgun caliber. Remington factory loads with a 150-grain round-nosed bullet produce a muzzle velocity of around 2,100 f.p.s. out of a 14-inch single-shot handgun barrel, for 1,470 foot-pounds of energy. A bigger 200-grain round-nosed soft-point factory load out of the same barrel will produce a muzzle velocity near 1,950 f.p.s. and nearly 1,700 foot-pounds of wallop. Out at 100 yards the 150-grain load would hit with about 1,200 foot-pounds of energy, while the heavier 200-grain bullet would still be good for nearly 1,300 foot-pounds. Like the old .30/30 Winchester, the .35 Remington's effectiveness as a handgun hunting cartridge can be significantly improved by handloading with bullets like the 180-grain .358-inch diameter Hornady "InterLock" spire-point bullet that has been designed specifically for use in single-shot handguns.

.308 Winchester

This cartridge was originally developed as the 7.62 NATO military round, but has enjoyed a fairly strong following among centerfire rifle shooters. Out of most quality long guns, the .308

Winchester sporting version has proven to be extremely accurate, and is now enjoying a growing popularity among handgun hunters.

Factory loads with 150- to 180-grain spire-point bullets will generally produce velocities of 2,200 to 2,500 f.p.s. at the muzzle of an T/C Encore 15-inch barrel. Hot handloads will up velocities to just over 2,500 f.p.s. with a 150-grain bullet. This will deliver 2,100 foot-pounds of muzzle energy. Downrange at 100 yards the load would punch a whitetail buck with more than 1,700 foot-pounds of remaining energy, and all the way out at 200 yards the bullet would still hit with close to 1,400 foot-pounds of energy.

.30/06 Springfield

A buck Larry Weishuhn dropped at just over 200 yards with his scoped .30/06 Thompson/Center Arms Encore and Federal 165-grain Nosler Ballistic Tip factory load was hammered with more than 1,800 foot-pounds of big-buck-taking energy. Fired from a 24-inch rifle barrel, this load is good for around 2,820 f.p.s., but out of the 15-inch Encore barrel the bullet exits the muzzle at just over 2,600 f.p.s., with around 2,475 foot-pounds of energy. At 100 yards the load drives home at around 2,420 f.p.s. with 2,100 foot-pounds of punch. Even good handloads cannot improve much on these ballistics.

Other Favored Rifle Cartridges for Handguns

Quite a few other centerfire big-game rifle cartridges are now showing up on the list of calibers available in a number of single-shot and bolt-action handguns. Among the more popular are the .223 Remington, .22-250 Remington, .243 Winchester, .260 Remington, .270 Winchester, 7mm-08 Remington, and .444 Marlin. When choosing a handgun specifically for hunting whitetails and other similarly sized game, keep in mind that the lighter bullet weights for some of these calibers simply do not deliver the energy levels needed for reliable game-taking performance. This is especially true when attempting a 200-yard shot.

Choosing a Whitetail Handgun

Before choosing a style or type of handgun for your whitetail hunting, first take time to look at the distances you're apt to be faced with shooting from, the thickness of the cover you hunt most and particularly the hunting regulations governing the use of handguns for deer in your state or the state where you will be hunting. All of these factors, plus a few others, will determine the caliber you should rely on to do the best, most efficient job of harvesting a big whitetail buck. And if it is one of the hotter, faster and flatter shooting centerfire rifle cartridges, it will definitely make your selection process easier.

These calibers are currently available only in handguns of either the single-shot or bolt-action design. Since the 1960s, Thompson/Center Arms of Rochester, New Hampshire, has dominated the break-open single-shot pistol market. And for good reason – they manufacture a very fine product at a reasonable price. In fact, they make two very fine handguns of this type – the Contender and the Encore. The Contender model is available with choice of a 10- or 14-inch barrel, while the Encore comes with either a 12- or 15-inch barrel. Both guns are of the break-open design, with the rear of the barrel hinging upward for easy insertion of the cartridge and removal of a fired case. Both models come with high-quality adjustable hunting sights, but feature easy installation of a long-eye-relief handgun scope. With the longer barrels these guns become quite a handful, weighing up to nearly 6 pounds with scope, base and rings. They are definitely more than a one-hand gun. A good rest always insures better accuracy.

The Lone Eagle from Magnum Research is another interesting and handy single-shot that's ideally suited for the big-game handgunner. Instead of the break-open design, this handful of whitetail-stopping power features a rotating or turret-type breech that's turned to open the chamber, allowing a cartridge to be easily slipped into the handgun. The gun comes with a 14-inch blued or chrome-finished barreled action and black synthetic stock. It is offered in most of the same calibers as the T/C single-shots.

There are several other big single-shots available that make fine whitetail handguns. The H-S Precision Silhouette Pistol and Wichita Arms Silhouette Pistol are two exceptional single-shot bolt-action designs that are available in a wide range of suitable big-game hunting calibers. However, hold on to your pocketbook with these two; prices can run from $1,500 to $2,000 for a standard model.

The Savage Arms Inc. bolt-action handgun known as the Striker is a much friendlier-priced whitetail-hunting handgun that's available in .223 Remington, .22-250 Remington, .243 Winchester, 7mm-08 Remington, .260 Remington, .308 Winchester and .300 WSM. The retail price for this 14-inch barreled bolt-action begins below $500 and features an internal box magazine that accommodates three backup rounds.

Revolver fans looking for a top-of-the-line big-bore deer gun can't do much better than the Ruger Stainless Redhawk in .44 Remington Magnum. This gun comes with choice of a 5½- or 7½-inch barrel, with scope rings and an integral scope mount milled into the rib of the barrel. But for those who prefer open sights, the revolver also features a ramp front blade and adjustable rear sight. For the hunter looking for a little more knockdown power than the .44 Magnum can muster, Ruger also offers their Super Redhawk Stainless in choice of .44 Magnum or .454 Casull. This model is offered with either a 7½- or 9½-inch barrel length. It too comes with the integral scope base and rings.

There are quite a few other big-bore revolvers equally suited for shots at whitetails out to around 100 yards, including the Smith & Wesson Model 629 Classic .44 Remington Magnum with 6½- or 8⅜-inch barrel; the Taurus Model 454 Casull in that caliber with choice of a 6½- or 8⅜-inch barrel; the Freedom Arms Model 555 Premier Grade in .44 Magnum, .454 Casull or the big .50 AE; and the Magnum Research BFR in .454 Casull, .444 Marlin, .45/70 Government or .50 AE. Of all the handguns currently available, it is those of the semi-auto design that have the least application as serious whitetail guns. While the current handgun market seems to be dominated by semi-autos in 9mm and .40 caliber/10mm for law enforcement and self-defense purposes, there are only a few self-loading handguns that are well suited for the whitetail woods.

Magnum Research offers several in one with their MARK XIX Component System that allows shooters to switch from .357 Magnum, .44 Magnum and .50 AE by simply swapping out barrel assemblies and magazines. For the serious whitetail hunter only the .44 Magnum and .50 AE will be of real interest. Barrels of 6- and 10-inch lengths are available for each caliber. Few other semi-auto handguns come close to matching the stopping power of this monstrous 6-pound handgun (with 10-inch barrel).

Hunting for whitetails with a handgun, especially when you've got your sights set on taking a trophy-class buck, isn't for everyone. Mastering a big-bore revolver or a break-open single-shot, bolt-action or semi-auto pistol well enough to keep hits in the vitals of a deer at your maximum effective range takes practice and exceptional shooting discipline. On the other hand, if hunting whitetails with a long-range centerfire rifle has lost some of its challenge, with a handgun a whole new world of deer hunting awaits you.

BIG BUCK WITH A HANDGUN

by Larry Weishuhn

Larry Weishuhn with his best-ever buck, which grossed 184 B&C points

I've taken many memorable whitetail bucks with a variety of handguns, but one old gnarly Texas buck I shot several seasons back stands out as one of the most unforgettable. While the deer was a buck any trophy hunter would be proud to claim, it was the performance of the pistol and the shot that I remember most.

After scouting the area, I found a spot where a big buck had been regularly working scrapes along the edge of a grassy field. A nearby piece of high ground offered a vantage point overlooking the field, and I quickly put together a ground blind. After a hard rain, a light drizzle set in, and lo and behold here came the buck, freshening his scrape line. Using a Stoney Point telescoping bipod, I rested the long-barreled .30/06 T/C Encore and waited until the buck turned broadside. I knew the range to be about 200 yards, and the 165-grain Nosler bullet would hit only an inch or so low. When the buck stopped, I squeezed back on the trigger. At the shot, the deer kicked high, then disappeared. I found him not more than twenty-five steps from where he stood at the shot. Just as impressive as the deer's many long points and two short kickers had been the performance of this handgun . . . at 210 long Weishuhn steps!

The success of this hunt can be largely attributed to the excellent downrange accuracy of this single-shot handgun and the performance of the hard-hitting Federal "Premium" cartridge. Even so, to build the confidence any hunter needs to attempt such a shot with a handgun requires spending plenty of time at the shooting bench with any handgun and load way before the season opens. It also helps to have the buck you're after well patterned.

Prior to actually going after this particular whitetail, I first did my homework, beginning with post-season scouting the previous winter to initially locate this same buck's old scrape line and travel routes. Then as the new season came and progressed, I spent a good deal of time glassing the field from a distance to keep from spooking this buck out of the area. When a rainy period set in, I realized it was the ideal time to hunt this deer, knowing the buck would be out to freshen his scrapes.

Prior to any hunting season, I spend a lot of time shooting the guns I'll be hunting with later, especially handguns. I want to know how the pistol groups at 100 yards, its trajectory and maximum effective distance. I then practice from positions I'm most likely to be faced with in the field. And whenever possible, I always shoot from crossed shooting sticks.

The best advice I can give to anyone looking at hunting whitetails with a handgun is to know its capabilities, as well as your own, before ever taking aim at deer. Having complete confidence in your handgun is the first step in becoming a successful handgun deer hunter.

Techniques
FOR
Record-Book
Bucks

Grunt 'em In

with Brad Harris

I t's amazing how many deer hunters spend a large part of their lives in the woods pursuing whitetails and never realize just how vocal deer can be. If you happen to be one of those hunters, don't feel bad. Many very respected deer-hunting experts have only tuned in to these sounds themselves during the last 20 years (or less). Now, calling deer has become a widely used tactic, and the number-one call used throughout whitetail country is the buck "grunt."

Noted deer-hunting authority Brad Harris, of Lohman game calls (Outland Sports), can be largely credited with the development of early commercially made grunt calls, now often referred to as grunt tubes. However, this quietly aggressive big-buck hunter is too modest to take credit for developing the technique for getting a buck in close.

"Before getting into the call business, I worked as a coal miner, and deer hunting was popular with most of us working at the Missouri mining operation. Several of the guys I worked with had experimented with trying to reproduce the grunting sound they often heard when a buck was chasing a doe, or on the prowl apparently looking for a doe. And they did this by simply pinching their noses and with their mouth making an 'awk' sound that was sort of brought up from the gut," recalls Harris.

This was during the mid-1970s, when few hunters were using grunt calls to lure in bucks, and none of the outdoor magazines were reporting on the technique. Harris became intrigued with the thought of actually "calling in a buck" and began practicing the sound, first witnessing its effectiveness during a bowhunt on one of Missouri's wildlife management areas in 1976.

"I had been hunting several days, and there weren't many other hunters on the wildlife management area, so when a 6-point buck began to pass my stand at about 80 yards, I decided to give the grunt a try. I pinched my nose and made a grunt, just like the guys at work had demonstrated. That buck stopped immediately, turned and came right to me! I was so flabbergasted, I shot completely over the deer at just 20 yards. But I had proven to myself that grunt calling worked," states Harris.

A few years later, Harris met legendary call maker Bill Harper and went to work for him at his Lohman game-call production facility. He found that this maker and a few others offered doe bleat calls and snort calls, but these didn't impress Brad as much as the sound of the buck grunt. So he began taking duck-call parts and assembling them to better reproduce the gutteral grunts he had heard bucks make during or just before the rut. And during the early 1980s, Lohman became the first call maker to offer a commercially produced grunt call. But Harris still had his work cut out for him – he had to convince the millions of deer hunters nationwide just how effective the call could be. And he was often faced with apprehension and resistance.

"I particularly remember a deer-hunting seminar I presented to the Missouri Bowhunters Association in either 1983 or 1984. When I finally got around to talking about the grunt tube – and demonstrated the call – the crowd of about three hundred practically rolled with laughter. It was the first time any of them had heard of using the call, and I found the same less-than-enthusiastic acceptance just about everywhere I made similar presentations. Things have certainly turned around and now I'm constantly informed by hunters they were using grunt calls 10 or 20 years before the first such calls showed up on the market," recalls Harris.

Today, just about everyone in the game-call-making business offers one or more grunt calls. As we'll see in the following portion of this chapter, grunt calls come in a variety of styles and sizes. While just 25 or 30 years ago only a very small handful of extremely woods-wise whitetail hunters realized that wary mature bucks could be lured into easy bow range with a few grunting sounds, the vast majority of bowhunters today, along with a growing number of modern gun and muzzleloading hunters, carry a grunt tube with them every time they head for the deer woods. The following are a few thoughts from Brad Harris about the use of these calls.

"The biggest mistake I see hunters making with grunt calls is that they simply don't use them enough. Perhaps they have run off a few deer and begin to doubt the effectiveness of the call and become scared to use it once they know a big buck is close, or in sight. To build confidence in these calls, you've got to use them!" exclaims Harris.

Harris also says that quite a few magazine articles have given readers bad advice about the use of a grunt call or grunt tube. One misconception is that a hunter should never call when the deer is looking his way. Wrong! Brad Harris believes in keeping that buck interested, keeping him from changing his mind. However, he says that success comes more often once the hunter learns how to correctly read deer – such as how the deer reacted to the initial call, where the deer's attention is focused, or what the buck is actually looking for.

Another bit of misinformation widely published in recent years has been that a hunter should not use a grunt call until he can actually see a buck. Harris says that nothing is farther from the truth. This master of the grunt call says that he will inevitably make a series of grunts whether he's seen deer or not. He believes that many hunters are so reluctant to use the calls that many good bucks pass by just out of sight, yet within hearing, and the hunter never knows they are anywhere near. A few grunts now and then can catch the attention of a buck on the prowl and bring him to where you're hunting.

"In my opinion, it's darn hard to overcall. I tend to lean more in favor of using the call rather than holding back and calling very conservatively," shares Harris.

Often this very successful big-buck hunter will begin calling with his grunt call, throwing in a few clashes with a set of rattling antlers, just as soon as he gets settled into his stand. Harris feels that making a series of natural buck sounds shortly after the walk into his stand is a great way to mask the light commotion he's just made. More than once his early grunting and rattling have resulted in a buck coming right to him.

The more grunt calls have been used since their early development only a few decades ago, the more hunters have learned about the best times to use them. Very experienced deer-calling authorities like Harris now realize that the calls can and will attract a buck just about any time during the fall

hunting seasons – from early fall well into winter. However, they have also come to realize that there are periods when the use of a grunt call enjoys a much higher rate of success.

"The greater the rut activity, the better grunt calls work!" states Harris. He adds, "During the pre-rut, many bucks are ready to breed, but the does haven't entered estrus. Still, the bucks are looking for a little action and are regularly on the prowl looking for a receptive doe, or another buck to scrap with to get rid of pent-up frustration. In my opinion, this is when bucks become the most vulnerable to the sounds of another buck's grunts."

He shares that the closer the pre-rut gets to the actual beginning of the rut, the more responsive the deer become to calling. There are times when the truly serious bowhunter will forsake practically everything else in order to be in a favorite treestand. The reason why is simple – as the deer activity picks up so does the chance of success.

"As the rut kicks into full swing and progresses, you may have to become more aggressive with your calling. I'm often asked if it is possible to call a buck away from a doe. Absolutely! It often just takes a little more work, combining a little rattling with your grunt calling to make that buck feel that competition is just over that rise, down that valley, or on the other side of that brush. It's a challenge to who controls this piece of territory," claims Harris.

He says that often the doe may take off at the sound of a second or third buck, wanting nothing to do with additional suitors. Harris feels this is the time to really challenge the buck and pour on some aggressive grunting. Even though he has enjoyed success calling a buck away from a hot doe, he acknowledges that the best time to call in a mature trophy-class whitetail during the height of the rut is when the buck is between does, when he's once again on the prowl and looking for another chance to breed.

This master of the grunt tube believes that many hunters simply call too lightly, with not enough volume to reach or get the attention of the deer. He feels that the volume of the calling should vary in relation to the weather conditions or the distance of the deer. It stands to reason that a hunter calling in the open country of Kansas should call louder than the hunter calling in a heavily wooded area with a much higher known deer density (deer per square mile). The closer the deer is to your stand, the lower the volume should be, about the same as when calling wild turkeys.

"If a buck hears your calls, chances are he will stop. Does that mean he'll come to you? No, but you've got his attention, and that's more than you probably had before you called. Find the right buck at the right time, and the chances are very good that he will come to investigate. And that's what keeps me using the grunt calls just about every time I climb into a deer stand," concludes Harris.

Making the Right Sounds

I can remember the first time I ever heard a buck grunt. Or rather I should say the first time I realized that the sound I was hearing was actually coming from a nice 8-pointer chasing a doe around in a field less than a hundred yards from my stand. Neck outstretched and nose a few feet from her tail, the 140-class 3½-year-old buck was sounding a rapid series of drawn-out and high-pitched grunts that sounded more like a high r.p.m. two-cycle motorcycle shifting gears than the sounds one would expect to hear coming from a whitetail.

Then, during a hunt a few years later, another mature buck that I guessed to be 3 or 4 years of age astonished me with a completely different grunt sound. Instead of the drawn out "yyyyyy-eeaapppppp" grunts of the buck I encountered earlier, this buck stood nearly motionless and sounded a deep popping sound. Although I had watched the deer approach the edge of a grown-up grassy opening, then stand to watch a smaller buck skirt the far edge of the woods clearing, it took me several minutes to realize that the sound was actually coming from that deer.

The calls at first were very drawn out, 5 to 10 seconds apart. Then, as the buck apparently became more agitated by the youngsters presence, the sounds grew closer together. And just before the 1½-year-old 6-pointer hurriedly disappeared into the deep woods to avoid a confrontation with the much larger buck, the popping grunts of the mature deer were spaced just a second or so apart. Every once in a while the buck would also throw in a short, deep "yyyeapp" grunt or two.

From these two completely different deer, each making a completely different grunt sound, I learned that for reasons that may be truly known only to the deer, whitetail bucks make different grunts to address different situations. The grunts I heard from the buck that pursued the hot doe are often referred to as "tending grunts," while the

grunts made by the second buck were apparently the more aggressive "challenge grunts" often made by an area's dominant buck when encountering a subordinate buck. (Whitetail expert Stan Potts will detail many of these different sounds on page 103.)

Knowing which kind of grunt to make and when is the real key to getting a buck to respond. Through most of the pre-rut and rut, short tending grunts are generally the best sounds to make, especially when you know the bucks in your area are on the prowl seeking a doe in estrus. However, if you're tying in some serious rattling of the antlers with your grunting, then it may be time to switch to challenge grunts, which can be the trick to lure the true monarch of an area into bow or gun range.

To make the lengthier tending grunt, place the mouthpiece of the call to your lips, cup one hand around the end of the flexible tube and lightly exhale into the call. It amazes me how many hunters try to "blow" a grunt tube like they would a duck or goose call. It takes far less air to operate a good grunt call. In fact, too much airflow will bottom out the loosely vibrating reed and not a sound, other than your huffing and puffing, will come from the call. Anything more than a slightly exaggerated exhale is too hard.

The tone of the grunt can be controlled some by placing the palm of the free hand up toward the opening of the call. By slightly opening and closing the hand that's cupped around the end of the flexible tubing, and by positioning the other hand right at the opening of the call, you can better control the clarity of the tones. With both hands relatively open, the notes are clear and sharper. Then the more the hands are used to cut off the sounds, the more muffled they become. Some hunters have discovered that by turning the end of the flexible tubing toward their chest, it is also possible to produce deeper-sounding tones.

The aggressive popping of a challenge grunt may take a little more practice. The basic "pop" can be easily reproduced with most grunt calls by simply exhaling a quick "ppffftt" of air into the call. The amount of air or the force of the exhale will vary from call to call, so practice this one at home long before you try it on a monster buck you've spotted near your stand. Then, once you can make the sound, work on the rhythm of a buck that's become more agitated. At first the challenge grunt may be just a simple series of individual pops, but as confrontation becomes more imminent a big mature buck will begin to put them together in a spaced-out series, with the pops growing closer together at the end.

The challenge grunt is one you may want to hold in reserve until you confirm that the deer you're calling is one of the more dominant bucks in the area. Use this call indiscriminately before seeing the buck and you may run off shooter bucks who simply are not interested in getting their butts kicked again! However, these subordinate bucks, which may still qualify for the Pope and Young archery record book or the Longhunter muzzle-loading records, are often the bucks that respond best to tending grunts.

When it comes to the amount of grunt calling you do, or the length of time between grunts or series of grunts, there are really no proven rules. There have been times when I've made a few grunts every 10 to 15 minutes, others when I may have used the grunt call only two or three times during an entire 3-hour stint in my treestand. And I've seen both approaches work. When calling to a buck that I can actually see, I watch the deer's body posture and degree of attention. I do my best to keep him interested, agitated or excited. But if he's making a beeline toward my stand, you can rest assured that the call has been put away and the bow or gun is in my hands.

Hunt whitetails long enough and you will sooner or later hear bucks make an unbelievable range of grunt sounds. Grunt back to these deer and many will hightail it in the other direction. But even that usually tells me there is a much better buck in the area and that I may be closer to a true trophy-class whitetail than I first realized.

Choosing a Grunt Call

Deer hunters are no different than any other group of enthusiasts of any other pursuit; we all have personal preferences in the equipment we use. These include the type, design or even size of the grunt call we hang around our neck or slip into a jacket pocket every time we take to the deer woods.

As simple as the grunt call concept may seem, and for as short a period as the technique has been in popular use, it's amazing at the variety of specialized grunt calls now available. In size they range from a call so big it could be mistaken for an elk-bugle tube to tiny devices that are held by the lips only. And for volume today's calls range from that of a small drum to the barely audible squeak of a small cabinet-door hinge. In tone the variety of grunt calls favored by hunters covers the spectrum

from the grunts of a young buck to those made by big, mature and barrel-chested bruisers. Some calls also feature multi-tone and variable-volume flexibility, which the hunter controls by simply depressing a small button or buttons positioned directly over the reed. In short, there is now a grunt call, or a good selection of grunt calls, to meet every whitetail buck hunting need.

Standard Grunt Call

The body of most grunt calls today varies little from the first such calls assembled by Brad Harris from duck-call parts. Some of these calls are made of wood, others of molded plastic. All feature a thin internal plastic reed that vibrates when blown to produce the grunt sound. And to make the calls more adaptable to a wider range of hunting situations, many of these calls now feature a tight-fitting rubber O-ring that can be moved along the reed to change the pitch and tone of the grunts, allowing the user to easily switch from the grunts of an older buck to those of a young buck, or somewhere in between.

In size, the bodies of these calls are usually around 4 to 5 inches in length, but commonly feature a 6- to 8-inch section of thin ridged plastic tubing attached to the exhale end. This tubing gives the call that deeper, from-the-gut sound. And with some models the tubing is expandable, meaning that it can be either shortened or lengthened by simply pushing it toward the call or pulling it away from the call. This will change the tone of the grunts without the caller having to pull the reed from the body to change it's position or slide a rubber O-ring back and forth on the reed.

Magnum Grunt Tubes

Older, mature whitetail bucks make a deeper, although not always louder, grunt than less mature bucks. To reproduce these sounds, some call makers are now offering so-called magnum grunt tubes that feature an enlarged sound chamber in the body or a longer and larger-diameter piece of flexible tubing extending from the call body. On some of these deep-sounding grunt calls this tubing becomes bigger toward the end, often ending in a megaphone-shaped bell.

Micro Grunt Tubes

Just as the name implies, these calls are much smaller than the standard grunt calls. In fact, calls of this

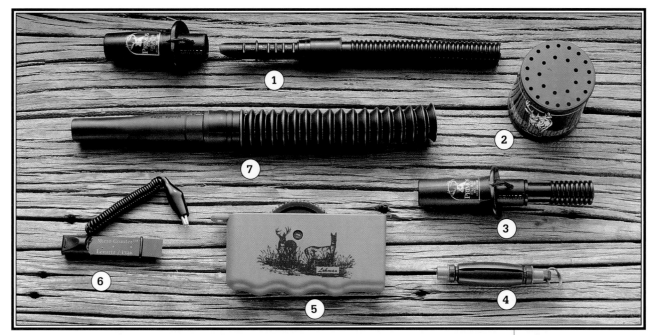

Different types of calls include (from top left): (1) adjustable grunt tube, (2) can call, (3) bleat call, (4) snort call, (5) hand-operated grunt call, (6) micro grunt call, (7) hyperventilator grunt call.

type have been designed so they can actually be operated "hands free." To use most micro grunt calls, the hunter simply holds the call in place with the lips and either inhales or exhales to produce the desired grunts.

One real advantage of a micro grunter is that most designs feature an elastic and self-retracting spiral plastic lanyard. The call is attached to an outer garment. When a bowhunter is ready to take his shot, the call can be released from the lips and will spring back out of the way to avoid getting caught by the bowstring. Another design actually attaches to the bow riser and is operated by sucking lightly on a piece of soft rubber tubing that is clipped to the bowstring. The design allows the hunter to make one or two more calls to insure the buck is in the right position before releasing the arrow.

A disadvantage of these tiny grunt calls is that they are basically only close-range calls. On typical hunting days with a light 5- to 10-m.p.h. breeze, it's doubtful that a buck beyond 75 yards would even hear most of these calls. But for getting that buck in really close, a micro grunter makes a fine back-up to a standard or magnum grunt call.

Variable-Tone Grunt Calls

One of the more recent trends in buck grunt calls are those that have multi-tone or even multi-call capability. While the designs vary from one make and model to another, all operate on a similar principle. When pressure is applied to the reed it changes its tone; the greater the amount of pressure applied the higher the pitch. This tone change works the same as the sliding O-ring found on adjustable standard models, only the sound of the call can be changed without sliding the call apart. Instead, pressure is applied to the reed by depressing a small button (or buttons) on the outside of the call body, or by pushing down on a rubber surface which in turn makes contact with the reed, or by twisting the rear of the call to tighten contact with the reed.

Quick-change variable-tone calls can add a sense of realism when grunts are combined with a rattling sequence. They allow the hunter to make two different toned-grunts, to sound more like two different deer. Some of these grunt calls also allow the hunter to make doe and fawn bleats with a little practice.

GRUNT CALLS WORK!

by Brad Harris

Brad Harris with evidence that grunt calls work

There are times when it's next to impossible to be absolutely quiet when walking in to your stand. Sometimes the route will take you through heavy brush, or across a woods floor covered with a heavy blanket of dry fallen leaves. At those times you might as well be walking across a heavy layer of corn flakes! Every step crunches so loudly you know that every deer within hearing knows you're in the woods, or so it seems to you.

Producing whitetail hunting videos means that in addition to packing in all of my normal hunting gear, I'm also faced with getting a camera, a mount that attaches to the tree or stand to steady that camera, a cameraman and often a second stand for the cameraman into the woods with as little commotion as humanly possible. Once I've gotten settled into my stand and have the cameraman in place and ready to tape right over my shoulder, I will more often than not follow up with a series of grunts and some rattling to add some natural buck sounds to the noise we may have made getting into our stands.

I don't really expect a buck to come running right in, but I feel that reproducing these natural sounds whitetails make may take the edge off of deer that heard us on our way to the stand site or while we were setting up. Even so, more than

once I've had a buck show up within a half-hour of my initial calling sequence.

One hunt really stands out in my mind. We knew of several really good bucks in our hunting area, and had already set up my stand and the camera stand days earlier. Still, the dry ground cover made for less-than-quiet walking as the cameraman and I made our way in for an afternoon/evening hunt. As soon as the camera was in place, I prepared to do some grunting and rattling to mask the noise we had made.

With rattling horns held ready in one hand and grunt call in the other, I decided to begin with a few aggressive grunts, then follow up with a minute or two of fierce horn rattling. Just as the notes of the second or third grunt died away, I nearly fell out of the stand when a beautiful Pope and Young class 8-pointer stood up from some tall grass only a couple of hundred yards from the stand. The deer looked in my direction, then without hesitation came on at a fast walk.

By the time I had slowly hung the rattling horns on a nearby branch, put the grunt tube away and picked up my bow, that buck was in range. The deer offered an easy shot. The cameraman got some great footage of a fine buck being taken with a bow, and I realized then more than ever before just how well grunt calling does work.

Rattling
Is Not Just for Texas

with David Hale

No one really knows when the first hunter rattled a set of whitetail antlers together and lured another buck within shooting range. However, in modern times we know that the tactic was widely used in the brush country of south Texas long before it began to catch on elsewhere in the country. Today trophy-minded whitetail-buck hunters from Mexico to Canada would no more think about heading for the deer woods without a set of rattling horns thrown over their shoulder than they would without their rifle, muzzleloader or bow.

David Hale, who co-founded Knight & Hale game calls with his equally well-known partner Harold Knight, is recognized as one of today's most successful trophy-buck hunters. In fact, much of this very successful line of game calls caters to the whitetail-deer hunter. And Hale is one of the strongest advocates of the use of rattling to get an old buck's attention.

"Deer are a lot like schoolboys. When a fight breaks out, they want to watch. They want to see who the champion will be. And this applies to everything from a button buck to the head honcho," states Hale.

While he makes this comment jokingly, he knows that he's never made a more true statement about the curiosity of the whitetail buck. However, this veteran whitetail hunter also recognizes that there's a lot more to rattling in a mature buck than simply walking into the woods and beating two antlers together. First, you must be in an area where there is a buck.

Hale says actively worked scrapes are one of the best indicators that a buck is in the general area. He says to keep in mind the true reason or purpose of a scrape, to mark and establish territory. Two intruder bucks clashing horns together in the vicinity of a resident buck's scrapes are sure to get his attention, and if everything else is right, Hale says the commotion could bring that buck on at a dead run.

Older, mature bucks may not respond as immediately or as thoughtlessly as younger subordinate bucks. Ever-cautious seasoned monarchs will very often slip in like a ghost, generally standing back from where the rattling and calling sounds are coming from in an attempt to see what's going on before coming in all the way. Hale knows that the type of buck he's looking to take is no dummy, and will regularly move downwind of his calling location to try to catch the scent of the other deer the buck cannot see. If he does move downwind, that buck will likely pick up the human odor of the hunter. To greatly reduce the chances of being winded by a trophy buck, David Hale chooses his calling locations carefully, and often in advance.

"When preparing to rattle in an area, I will place a portable treestand days before I actually hunt the area. By doing so, I can slip into the area and put a hunting partner in the stand, while I remain on the ground to rattle and call. More than once I have had wise old bucks circle downwind of my calling position in order to test the air currents. My partner who is in the treestand above me can see the responding deer before I do – if I ever do," remarks Hale.

This experienced trophy-buck hunter feels that rattling tends to be considerably more successful when the caller is positioned on the ground. For that reason, David uses rattling more often when hunting with a partner than when hunting alone. Due to the exceptional eyesight and hearing of the whitetail, he feels that the caller needs to rely on some type of concealment to keep from being detected by an approaching buck, which could appear from almost any direction.

"When hunting solo, I prefer to use the rattling antlers more sparingly than when hunting with a partner. I believe if a buck is in a responsive mood, he will respond without a lot of rattling, but the sounds of antlers clashing together is a good initial attention getter. Experience has shown me the ears and eyes of a whitetail are to be respected more than some folks think!" exclaims Hale.

Rattling technique will vary from hunter to hunter, and there's really no right way or wrong way to rattle. There is no research to support the idea that a big set of antlers works more effectively than a small set when rattling. However, Hale points out that the biggest mistake many hunters make while rattling is to become so caught up in the rattling sequence they forget one very important element of the technique, movement. Instead of watching for the buck they're trying to call, many pay far too much attention to the rhythm of the antlers and how the tines interlock with one another. While they watch how the antlers work, the buck could be watching them.

Hale is a firm believer in mixing grunt calls with his rattling, especially just before bringing the horns together for his initial sequence. He points out that before actually locking antlers, mature bucks will often posture for one another in an attempt to intimidate each other. The deer commonly approach each other with a stiff-legged, sideways walk, with ears laid back and the hair on the back of their necks bristled up. The bucks more often than not accompany this mannerism with a wide range of guttural grunts, often throwing in hissing or spitting sounds. And even once they've locked horns, many times they continue to make some of these noises. Adding such sounds to your rattling sequences can add one more touch of realism.

Hale keeps his rattling sequences short, explaining, "Hunters must remember that when a deer responds to a rattling sequence, it has the hunter's location pinpointed. This is why it is so important to be conscious of every movement. If we are continually banging antlers, we are creating excessive movement. This is the reason I keep my rattling sequences very short in length."

A routine that tends to work for him is to begin with a couple of loud grunts with one of his Knight & Hale Extenda-Tone grunt calls. Then David will snap a few branches just before he begins to work the antlers. This initial rattling lasts for about a minute.

"While I work the antlers, I will kick or stomp the ground with my foot to simulate the pounding of the bucks' hooves," adds Hale. Almost as soon as he ends the antler rattling, he follows up with a couple of additional loud grunts, then goes totally silent for a few minutes, maybe as long as 10 minutes. This allows him to listen for the sound of a deer that may be charging in. If a buck happened to be only a few hundred yards away, that deer could be right on top of him in a minute or two.

"Most of the time, I'll hear a deer before I ever see it. Hunters should realize most of the deer that respond are going to be coming in a hurry. Though this is not always the case, a very high percentage of the time it is," remarks Hale.

David Hale likes to mix in grunt calls whenever he rattles.

Rattling is now a time-proven tactic for luring in big, mature bucks, whether they're hunted in Texas, Saskatchewan or Illinois. Hale feels that the only way a hunter will ever learn if rattling works in his area is to get out and try it. And he will be the first to warn that what works so well one day will very likely fail to get the attention of anything the next.

"In my opinion, this alone is what makes hunting the whitetail deer so much fun – and this magnificent animal so great. If there was a surefire method for calling deer, I don't believe we could call it hunting anymore," concludes David.

Rattlin' Gear

The simple fact is that it doesn't take a lot of extra gear to successfully rattle for whitetails. In addition to the equipment you already use, at most it may require a set of "rattling horns" or a "rattling bag" or some sort of other hand-operated call that simulates the sound of antlers clashing together. If you haven't already been using a grunt call, you may also need one of these in order to make the staged fracas sound more like two mature bucks whipping the daylights out of each other.

Just about everyone in the game-call business these days offers rattling devices in the form of hardwood-dowel-filled cloth bags or synthetic (fake) rattling antlers. The following sections will take a look at some of these.

Rattle Bags

These handy little calling devices take up very little room and can be easily slipped into a jacket pocket or day pack. Most are simply a cloth bag loosely filled with extremely hard oak dowel rods of irregular square and triangular shapes. To use a rattle bag, the hunter can either roll it back and forth between both hands, or allow it to hang from one side and with a free hand roll it back and forth on the side of that leg. The one-handed operation allows the hunter to keep his bow or gun ready in the other hand, or work a grunt call simultaneously.

When selecting a rattling bag, choose one with a moderately thin (but tough) cloth bag, like the Knight & Hale Ultimate Rattle Bag, which features a convenient belt loop for hanging on the side. A bag made of a heavy nylon-type material could muffle the sounds of the dowel rods inside. Also, try feeling the shape of the oak dowels. If they are even slightly rounded, they won't produce the "pops" and "clatter" needed to sound like the

antlers of two bucks meshing their headgear together.

When worked by an experienced rattler, these bags can sound surprisingly realistic. In addition to the Knight & Hale bag mentioned above, Primos Game Calls, Quaker Boy and Hunter Specialties also market similar products.

Real Deer Antlers

No one relishes the thought of cutting up a prized whitetail rack to obtain a set of actual antlers for rattling. One alternative is to get out in late February and early March (in most whitetail country) to spend some time looking for shed antlers. Not only is this a great way to get a set of rattling antlers that will mean more to you, but it also allows you to get a better feel for how many of the ol' big boys made it through the season and the winter. And it also allows you to find buck sign and travel corridors you probably never even knew to exist. If you simply don't have the time to get out, maybe you can buy a set of antlers or sheds.

Guys, if you really want to make your wife or girlfriend happy, next spring when everyone is cleaning out their garages and holding yard sales, spend a few weekends taking her to them. Sooner or later, you're likely to find a nice set of antlers lying on a table with a $10- to $20-pricetag on them. Just try to act surprised that you ever found such a treasure. You don't want to blow your cover.

Synthetic Rattling Antlers

Several manufacturers have gone to a great deal of trouble to have molds made from real whitetail antlers in order to produce synthetic casts that look surprisingly like real antlers. Other call makers have simply turned out various colored plastic rattling antlers with forks and tines that look very little like the real thing. But looks are not what's important. Sound is. Some of the plastic materials used to make rattling antlers of this type have a soft, dead sound. Before buying any set of synthetic antlers, work them and listen to the tone. It needs to be sharp and crisp, not like two plastic dinner plates rattled together.

Other Hand-Held Devices

One of the finest rattling calls ever made is the Dynamite Rattler from Lohman Game Calls. This call consists of six rectangular-shaped hard-plastic sticks somewhat loosely bound together by an elastic band at each end. A hole that runs full-length through the center of the 6-inch-long sticks, plus the grooves that run along the outside of each flat surface result in unique sound resonation. This call has the tones of real antlers being banged together. It is operated just like a rattling bag, but it has no cloth bag to inhibit the sound, hold human odor or rip and wear out. A number of other hand-held devices made of hard plastic have come and gone over the years, but this call will be around for some time. It works. 🦌

WOOD, PLASTIC OR THE REAL THING?

by Toby Bridges

Wind gusts of 20 to 30 m.p.h. rocked the treetops as I slowly made my way down a long wooded Iowa ridge toward a hot stand with lots of promise of producing a shot at a record-book buck. A strong cold front was pushing into the area, and the weatherman predicted a heavy rain later that night and temperatures the next day well below normal. I'm not a real fan of hunting in such windy conditions, but the timing of the approaching rut told me I needed to get in that stand for the afternoon.

I was about 150 yards from the stand when I heard something banging. The sounds came now and then, two or three well spaced flat-sounding bangs, followed by a series of raking pops. I knew it couldn't be bucks fighting. The sounds were just too unrealistic. If someone else was hunting my stand and rattling, they sure sounded terrible. But the sounds were definitely coming from the vicinity of the stand I had hung a week earlier.

Slowly, I approached the stand and almost laughed to myself when I spotted the source of the sounds. Flapping in the wind was the wide nylon-webbed strap of the safety belt I had left attached to the tree, with the plastic buckle continuously hitting against the aluminum stand. "Great, that noise has probably spooked every deer for miles!" I thought to myself.

Then, as I eased to within 50 yards of the stand, a movement off to my right caught my attention. And I turned my head just in time to watch as a monstrous Boone and Crockett class whitetail buck spun and hightailed it down the side of the ridge. To this very day I still wonder if that buck had responded to the sounds of that buckle hitting the metal stand, mistaking it for two other bucks locking horns.

Today's hunting market is filled with an almost unbelievable variety of synthetic rattling antlers, wooden dowel-filled rattle bags, and other hand-held and operated calls for simulating two bucks fighting. And many of those who use these rattling aids have reported a reasonable amount of success with them. However, for my rattling, nothing beats the sound of the real thing – a good set of antlers.

For years I relied on a couple of solid, sound sheds picked up early in the winter. Then one season I shot a good 130-class buck during the late muzzleloader season, and really had no intention of mounting the head. So I sawed the horns at the base from the skull, and whacked off the brow tines. The result is a great-sounding set of rattling antlers that I've used for more than 10 years.

Another set of "rattling horns" that have proven to be ideal came from a 130- to 140-class mule deer I shot in Wyoming one fall. The buck never did have brow tines, and since the antlers fork high on the first tine, then again near the tips, all of the sharp points are out away from my hands.

When you're relying on the real thing to put together a set of rattling antlers, it really doesn't matter if a pair of sheds match. Many successful hunters carry a set of antlers comprised of sheds from the same side. When using sheds that have been picked up in the woods or fields, just be sure they are sound and solid. Most times, rodents will completely consume dropped antlers for their calcium content before spring sets in, or at least gnaw on them until they are no longer suitable for rattling. However, I have found sheds that were 2 or 3 years old. These are usually very weather checked and dried out. When two of these are used to rattle, they produce a "dead" sound. Fresh sheds or antlers cut from a harvested buck will have a clear, sharp tone. Whether or not it really makes a difference to the deer, it sounds better to me, and these are the only "rattling horns" I'll carry into the woods.

TECHNIQUES FOR RECORD-BOOK BUCKS

Using Common Scents

by Toby Bridges

Whitetails are a product of their environment. They have learned to live right in our backyards, often without us even knowing it, by becoming fully dependent on all five senses – hearing, taste, touch, sight and smell. If any one sense is adversely affected, deer will readily relocate to an area that's better suited to their daily routines.

Humans cannot definitively determine which of a whitetail's senses are the most acute, or which is of most importance to the deer's survival. However, whitetail hunters will readily agree that of the five senses, a deer's sense of smell is the animal's number-one line of defense. The sight of a person walking along the edge of an open field or the sound of man working in his yard or on the farm will not send deer into flight nearly as quickly as the subtle scent of a human wafting along in the gentle air currents.

Smell has to be one of the primary senses the whitetail deer relies on each and every day of its life. Among those hunters who spend much of each fall in deer woods, it is an accepted fact that a deer can pick up the scent of a human upwind for more than a mile. At one time or another, all deer hunters have been busted by deer passing downwind of our stands.

Just as a deer's sense of smell serves as its first line of defense, it is also likely a whitetail's primary means of communication. The whitetail is a living, walking bundle of messages. Glands are located between the hooves of all four feet (interdigital glands), along the insides of both back legs (tarsal glands), on the outside of each hind leg between the knee and foot (metatarsal glands), at the lower corner of the eyes (pre-orbital glands), and at the base of each antler (forehead glands). The scent from each of these glands can send an important message to other deer, from the urgency to breed to the need to flee.

The next time you harvest a whitetail, whether it's a buck or doe, take a few minutes to examine the deer before field-dressing it. There is not a better time to learn where a whitetail's scent glands are located. Here's where to look and what to look for.

Locating and Identifying Whitetail Scent Glands

Tarsal Glands

Easily the most recognized of all deer glands, the tarsal gland can be found on the inside of each hind leg, near the middle joint. The hair of the tarsal gland is longer than other hair on the inside of the leg, and on a rutting buck the hair is usually much darker in color, making the tarsal gland

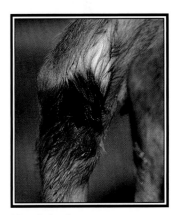
Tarsal gland

relatively easy to locate. If in doubt, just follow your nose. During the rut, tarsal glands are usually quite pungent.

The actual glands are found directly under the skin. Secretions known as *lactones* are carried to the hairs of the tarsal gland through the hair follicles. Experts tend to agree this gland is a whitetail's most important communication gland. Many game biologists claim that the tarsal gland produces the scent that establishes a whitetail's place in deer society, including its sex, age and even physical condition. In essence, the tarsal gland is the deer's fingerprint.

Metatarsal Glands

On the outside of each hind leg, located between the foot and mid-leg joint, you'll find the metatarsal gland. It looks like a small oval-shaped patch of white hair surrounding a small area of hairless skin. The function of this gland is not fully known. However, some researchers feel that it serves as something of a thermostat, helping to regulate a whitetail's body temperature. Others feel that the metatarsal gland's purpose is to leave scent on the ground while the deer is bedded, while still others believe that its purpose has nothing to do with scent, but rather the detection of light vibrations in the ground.

Interdigital Glands

Look for the interdigital gland between the toes of all four hooves. It can be identified as a small, sparsely haired, sac-like feature. It is a highly fragrant gland that leaves scent on the ground each time a whitetail takes a step, allowing deer to track one another. Most whitetail biologists feel that each deer has its very own scent, which is deposited by the interdigital glands, and that deer can positively identify the footsteps of one another through the scent left by these glands. It is believed that bucks often trail a specific doe during the rut entirely through the scent left by these glands. When whitetails pound their front feet against the ground while trying to identify a foreign object or odor, they are depositing large amounts of interdigital gland secretion, which many experts feel warns other deer of possible danger.

Forehead Glands

These are probably the hardest of all whitetail glands to locate and positively identify. However, the secretions from these glands are generally believed to be the reason that the hairs of a buck's forehead, near the base of each antler, are commonly darker than surrounding hairs. A few whitetail experts have likened the scent left from forehead glands to that buck's personal business card. The scent helps to establish an individual buck's position in the pecking order for the breeding season.

Preorbital Glands

These glands are also known as the *lacrymal* glands and can be identified as the tear ducts located directly in front of each eye. On live deer, or those just harvested, you'll notice a yellowish or whitish waxy secretion in and around a tiny slit just forward of the eye. Bucks deposit the scent from the preorbital glands on overhanging limbs, usually near or in conjunction with a scrape.

When to Use Scents

"A deer's sense of smell is over 100 times greater than a human's. The nose structure of whitetail deer gives them the ability to pick up odors a human cannot detect. They continually monitor the air for scent particles. Wind, temperature and the amount of moisture in the air all affect scent and how it travels through the air. Ideal scenting conditions exist in a humidity of 20 to 80 percent, a temperature of 40 to 90 degrees and light breezes up to 15 miles per hour," states noted outdoor writer Monte Burch.

While the deer hunter has his work cut out for him to avoid detection by the whitetail's sensitive nose, this same keen sense of smell can be put to work to attract deer as well. Properly used at the proper time, doe-in-heat scents or buck-in-rut-based urine can work amazingly well. Used improperly, or at the wrong stage of the season, these same scents can also throw up a red flag, especially if every hunter in the woods is freely splashing the stuff all over the place.

Knowing the stage of the pre-rut, rut or post-rut is important to determine which hunting scent to use. Most commercial scent suppliers offer a variety of deer-hunting scents, or lures. Some are simply natural deer scents that may have absolutely nothing to do with breeding. These include non-rut buck and doe urine, forehead scents, etc., which simply add the natural odor of deer to your hunting area. Then there are the rut-based scents, including doe-in-estrus and rutting buck urine, which will definitely spice up either a scrape made naturally by a deer or a man-made mock scrape. And there are the food scents intended to attract deer, and cover scents to help hide human odor.

Occasionally, I will utilize a rut-based urine to add a little appeal to a scrape. Scents should be used with caution if you are targeting trophy deer. With so many hunters utilizing such a wide range of natural and synthetic deer scents, I find it works better to go as scent free as possible and hunt the natural movement of the deer in my area. This tactic includes taking the time to wash my hunting clothes in scent-free laundry detergents; showering with scent-free soaps; spraying boots, gloves and other gear down regularly with scent-killing odor neutralizer; and then avoiding all contact with anything that could take a foreign, deer-alerting odor to my stand location.

KEEP YOUR COOL . . . AND YOUR NOSE INTO THE WIND

by Harold Knight

Harold Knight

Controlling our scent is a vital element in successful deer hunting. I'm always very conscious of wind direction and my scent while hunting, especially during extremely warm temperatures. I take every precaution to keep my clothing very clean and use odor eliminators religiously during these periods.

I work hard through the summer months to locate nice bucks to hunt come fall. I know well that when one of these deer gets a nose-full of my scent, he is going to become even harder to hunt than he is already. For that reason, I avoid hunting my prime areas until the temperature cools down. In most cases, I use warm-weather periods to prepare myself for when the time becomes right. Hunting big deer is a game of odds – and I only gamble when the odds are in my favor.

There are times, however, when I'll use my scent to swing those odds in my direction. For instance, I love to go after a trophy buck that's taken refuge in a standing cornfield. Allowing that buck to wind me is an important step toward successfully getting a shot.

I'll wait until the sun is fully up for a couple of hours, giving the deer plenty of time to bed down in the cornfield. This, I believe, greatly increases my chances of encountering more deer while in the standing corn. Also, by mid-morning there's usually a nice breeze blowing. I use this in several ways.

First, the wind helps me by creating noise as it rattles the dried corn leaves. The noise helps cover any sounds I make while moving amongst the dried cornstalks. The second way the wind helps me is that it alerts the deer to my presence and distracts them. By circling the upwind end of the field, I allow the air currents to carry my scent into the field before I begin hunting. The deer focus on the scent and I enter from the opposite, downwind side. If there is only a light or moderate breeze, I place pieces of cloth with my scent on them among the standing cornstalks upwind of where I figure the deer to be. This keeps my scent flowing into the field while I'm stalking through it – from the opposite direction.

Once in the corn, I travel very slowly, listening for the sounds of deer among the dried corn. I am also consistently crouching, looking for the legs of deer standing in nearby cornrows. As I move along these rows, I periodically produce one or two soft "gruu-nnts" with my grunt call. This, I feel, not only serves as a possible attractor for a nearby buck, but masks the sounds of a human. By moving slowly, and sounding like a deer among the corn, I often get into very close range of my targets. I have arrowed a couple of my top trophies within mere feet inside these havens.

USING SCENTS PROPERLY

by John Collins

John Collins and a heavy-beamed whitetail

Some hunters have told me that they have had mixed results using scents (both masking scents and deer lures). When you work with animals as edgy, spooky and high-strung as a whitetail, you must choose a quality scent product and use it properly. The following factors all come into play and have an effect on hunter success using scents: wind speed, thermals, deer density, buck/doe ratio, quality and type of scent, hunter's ability to place scents, hunter cleanliness, and time of year. Obviously, you can't control all of these factors, but you must consider each of them every time you enter the deer woods.

Far too many outdoor writers have misled hunters with statements like, "Any amount of human odor will spook deer." This is just plain wrong. Odor concentration is the key. Deer will accept a lot more in-direct human odor than you might realize. A buck analyzes the odor to determine its strength to see if danger is present. A weak human odor is often acceptable because the deer thinks the danger has passed.

Your direct human odor is the most likely to

spook deer and also the toughest odor to mask. The next biggest problem areas are your entry and exit trails to your hunting spot. Here's how to put the odds in your favor.

For starters, shower with scent-free soap prior to going hunting if at all possible. Your odor will be considerably weaker to deer if you do. Wear clean camo that hasn't accumulated sweat and bacteria, and wear rubber boots that come up at least to your ankles. Light rubber or latex gloves that you can work in are also an asset when handling scent sticks or boot pads.

Spray an odor-eliminating product like my "No Scent" on your hair and camo prior to entering your hunting area. Do not brush up against branches and trees as you approach your hunting spot. As you press against trees and limbs, you push your odor into these heavy objects. When you reach your hunting spot, sit in the middle of two cashew-sized amounts of a quality masking (cover) scent. Two of my favorites are my Fox Plus Concentrate or Tree Top Raccoon Gel. Put masking scent on two pieces of bark or sticks, and place one at shoulder height on one side of you and another waist-high on your other side. It is very important to sit in the middle of the two! Do not place masking scents more than 2 feet away from you. Masking scents should also be placed on your boots to disguise your entry and exit trails.

As a rule, the more precautions you take, the better off you will be. Everyone will get "winded" at times, but if your masking scent confuses a buck long enough for a shot, it has done its job. Also, remember that the windier the weather is, the harder it is to stay undetected.

Many hunters have misconceptions about how whitetails detect deer lures (attractants). They feel that if a buck comes downwind of a lure but doesn't stop and come to it, the lure wasn't any good. But there could be several explanations for this result.

The biggest problem with a lure is getting it to the animal's nose. This can be difficult to do, and many hunters fail to do it successfully. For example, the wind might be favorable when you set up and get on stand, but it can switch or die-down at any time, affecting the travel of your lure's scent. Your lure placement may be too low or too high, and the concentration may be too sparse or too heavy. For example, a buck that crosses a lure's scent trail with his head held high may not wind it if the lure was placed only on the forest floor.

How can you tell if a buck has really winded your lure? Simple, you will usually see a visual response. Ideally, he will stop and then walk toward the scent source. But you may see other reactions. The buck might stop, face the wind, and simply satisfy his curiosity from a distance. Or, he may get edgy if the scent smells wrong or it's too strong. Finally, he may spook if the scent is a poor-quality product or has spoiled due to poor preservation, old age or excessive heat.

Sometimes a hunter is sure a buck has gotten wind of his lure, but the animal shows no interest in it. Chances are that the lure consists only of straight (non-estrus) deer urine. How many times a day does a buck smell straight deer urine or interdigital gland scent? Enough to make them both poor attractants. Straight deer urine has little attraction or "holding" capability and will give you little or no response. Yet it's the only ingredient in the majority of buck lures on the market today.

Because straight deer urine performs so poorly, I use only "in-season" urines in my formulated lures. These urines are collected during the rutting season and contain concentrated chemical compounds that induce sex responses and other natural responses in big game. I believe that in formulation with other natural materials, such as musks and glands, these urines produce the best attractants.

If you are having problems with masking scents and deer lures working as well as advertised, try altering your scent placement methods and concentrations. That will usually make all the difference in the world – provided you're using a quality scent product.

John Collins is the founder of James Valley Scents, whose products can be purchased by calling 1-800-DER-LURE or writing to:

John Collins
James Valley Scents
38853 SD HWY 20
Mellette, SD 57461

Bill Jordan with one of the many bucks he harvested by knowing where deer feed

TECHNIQUES FOR RECORD-BOOK BUCKS

The Secret to Finding Deer
Is Through Their Stomachs

with Bill Jordan

Hundreds of magazine articles are written annually expounding upon the idea that hunters need to spend great lengths of time in the deer woods throughout the year in order to fully understand whitetails' seasonal patterns and to scout for trophy-class bucks. And there isn't one recognized deer-hunting expert featured in this book who would totally disagree with such efforts.

Still, many of these very successful big-buck hunters are now spending less time patterning and scouting for the deer they hunt, simply because these hunters have learned exactly where to begin their annual searches for that next trophy-class whitetail. Bill Jordan, the founder of Realtree and Advantage camouflage patterns, begins his season or hunt by first identifying and locating the primary food sources in his hunting areas.

"Locate those food sources, and you'll find the deer . . . it's that simple!" claims Jordan.

Whitetails are extremely selective feeders, yet they dine on an unbelievable variety of plants. Various grasses tend to make up most of a deer's summer diet, but a whitetail's preference generally turns to mast crops as the fall season progresses and nature's bounty begins to ripen. Later, when the dead of winter sets in, hordes of whitetails often turn to agricultural crops for sustenance through the long, lean months. Knowing what the deer prefer to feed on and when can be the key to establishing the patterns and habits of the deer where you hunt.

Jordan feels that the better a hunter can identify primary food sources, and the closer they are to where he lives, the easier it will be for that hunter to establish a "home court advantage." He recommends that you try to learn as much as possible about the food sources on the properties adjacent to where you hunt as well. Deer do not realize property boundaries, and while some whitetails may be bedding and feeding right where you hunt, the majority of their movements could be off the property. But as long as you discover the travel routes, you'll always have the opportunity to establish a stand site and hunt these deer.

"Start early and follow their movements through the entire season. Early in the year I try to establish some summer feeding patterns; then I'll often position a stand off a ways from this daily routine and observe the deer through a good pair of binoculars.

Planting food plots can increase the number of deer in the area you hunt.

This allows me to get to know some of the deer without intruding into their domain," says Jordan.

Many times when early archery seasons open – in some states as early as late August or early September – whitetails are still on something of a summer feeding pattern. The hunter who carefully observes from a distance can often establish where the deer regularly enter and leave a soybean field, stand of clover, food plot or any other food source. Once these entries and exits are identified, a strategically positioned stand can result in a short hunt.

"If the food source happens to be a field, you may have to ease in deeper from the edge to determine the best stand site. Sometimes the best concentration of travel to and from the field may be a hundred to several hundred yards back from the field. When checking out these areas, create as little disturbance as possible. Don't push and don't take chances that could cause the deer to completely change their patterns," Jordan shares.

Jordan says that hunters should always try to locate obvious sign, such as big tracks, rubs and scrapes. These are the keys that indicate that a huntable buck or bucks frequent the area. Still, this knowledgeable hunter strongly feels that even big-buck sign will generally be found near a major food source.

"With experience, hunters will learn to read whitetail habitat. This includes learning which food sources the deer prefer at different times of the year. In time, the astute woodsman will also learn to identify deer sign that's nearby, and understand why it's there," he claims.

During the early season, bucks regularly band into bachelor groups, which could include a dozen or more mature whitetail bucks. It's not unusual to happen upon an area that's literally loaded with rubs. This is often where such a group tended to hang out as velvet-covered antlers began to harden and the deer were anxious to rid the new antlers of the drying velvet membrane. More often than not, these early rubs can be found close to an established food source, usually right along a field edge or not far from it.

Too often inexperienced hunters spend far too much time hunting late in the season near rubs that may be a month or two old. While a stand located inside a heavily rubbed area frequented by a band of bachelor bucks can be a real hot spot early in the season, those bucks have often vacated the area by the outset of the rut. This is especially true if the deer have moved to an entirely different

food source. Bill advises that learning to recognize fresh sign, such as rubs, scrapes and even big tracks, is an invaluable step in becoming a consistently successful buck hunter.

Even later on in the season, as the rut approaches and begins, the rubs and scrapes of older trophy-class whitetail bucks can generally be located within a very short distance of an active feeding area. Why? Jordan points out that while the bucks may become less and less interested in feeding at the height of the breeding period, other deer will continue to follow established feeding patterns – particularly the does that will be faced with a long gestation period once bred. Deer like to be around other deer, and this tendency is especially true of bucks looking for does that may be approaching or entering the estrus cycle. "Find the does and your buck will be close by!" he exclaims.

This well-known whitetail-hunting expert is lucky enough to hunt a half-dozen or more respected deer states each fall. However, when traveling to an area thousands of miles from his home in Georgia, Jordan doesn't always have the luxury of spending days afield to scout for sign and to pattern the deer he's there to hunt. Many times he must put his trust into the efforts of others to establish the movements of a good buck. But even then, he will very often forfeit a morning's hunt in order to glass a field from a distance to determine exactly where the deer enter and leave the food source. And it's at these points that he will usually begin his hunt that evening or the next morning.

However, Jordan admits that it is possible to have too much of a good thing. Where there are multiple food sources, pinpointing a concentration of sign can become more difficult and the deer harder to pattern. This is when the hunter who knows the whitetails' preferred foods and the times the deer tend to turn to these plants has the advantage.

"If you want to become a much better deer hunter, and to hunt with a higher probability of being in the right spot at the right time to get a shot at a trophy-class whitetail buck, then spend more time learning to identify those plants on which the deer in your area feed. Whitetails will readily leave one food source for another when the timing is right, when a more palatable mast crop or grain ripens or matures. Knowing when to hunt a certain food source can be just as important as reading sign, maybe more important," states Jordan.

In the following pages we will take a look at some of a whitetail's preferred food sources in different regions of the country and when to concentrate on them.

What Whitetails Eat

It would probably be just as easy, or possibly even easier, to cover what deer don't eat. Depending on where you live or where you hunt whitetails, these animals consume a wide variety of forage, much of which is not found throughout the whitetails' entire range. And oddly enough, deer in one region will readily eat and flourish on plants you could not force a deer to eat in another region, mainly since that food source may be totally foreign to the other area and its deer.

The main sources of nourishment for southern whitetails living deep in the heart of North Carolina's Dismal Swamp are different than the plants fed upon by northern whitetails found in the Illinois corn belt or prairie whitetails found in the hay fields of eastern Wyoming. No matter where your whitetail hunting takes you, learning the preferred food sources of that area or region will definitely up your odds for success.

The following section is not intended to be a complete look at all the grasses, forbs, fruits or grains deer regularly feed on, but it does include those that tend to be most favored or the most widely found. To better give you an insight into what deer feed on most in the area where you live or hunt, we'll break down the information by geographic region.

Northeast

This region is primarily made up of two forest types – huge expanses of spruce and fir in the northernmost stretches and wide, seemingly endless stands of hardwoods across the southern tier. Neither of these heavily forested areas offers much in the way of natural clearings.

Through late spring and most of the summer, whitetails within this region feed on a variety of grasses and leafy ground cover, including goldenrod, dandelion, milkweed, ragweed, crown vetch and clover. However, as these plants begin to "harden" with the approach of autumn, northeastern whitetails begin to turn to a wide range of woody browse. In fact, deer throughout most of this region become very dependent on food sources such as sumac, crabapple, dogwood, greenbriar, honeysuckle, rhododendron and dozens of other woody browse through most of the year. In many areas these are the only food sources available during the lean winter months. Here, it is often a matter of feeding on what's available rather than what's preferred.

But even though there may at first seem to be little to feed on selectively, deer will tend to show preferences. Where present, the new growth or twigs at the ends of sugar maple, yellow birch or black-cherry limbs can be among the first browse consumed by fall deer. And the ever-persistent green leaves still present on raspberry and blackberry briars often offer northeastern whitetail deer a tender, highly digestible food source into early October.

Throughout the middle portions of this region are sizeable pockets of hardwoods interspersed among heavy coniferous forests. When acorns, beechnuts and other hardwood mast crops begin to fall to the ground, they become whitetail magnets until the crop has been completely consumed. In the southernmost portions of this region, where hardwoods predominate, this mast crop becomes an increasingly important food source. The Northeast is known for its cold, brutal winters, and deer will readily feed on an abundant acorn crop. This is partially because they tend to show a preference for the taste of acorns and partially because of the biological need to consume a rich, digestible food that converts to fat in preparation for winter survival.

Along the southern edge of this region is an agricultural belt, with corn and hay crops such as clover, alfalfa and timothy farmed as a source of feed for a major dairy industry. These crops, along with the fruits produced by numerous orchards, can attract large numbers of deer at certain times each fall and winter.

Northern Great Lakes

This region primarily consists of heavy forests surrounding the great lakes, made up of southern Ontario and the upper halves of Minnesota, Wisconsin and Michigan. Here boreal spruce and fir forests blend southward into pines and northern hardwoods. While conifers dominate most of this area, especially the farther north a hunter travels, pockets or stands of hardwoods can be found throughout much of the region.

Agricultural crops are scarce and browse is the primary food source for whitetails throughout much of the Northern Great Lakes region. In fact, for much of this area, browse is the only food source for nearly half of the year. High-preference winter foods include American mountain ash, mountain maple, serviceberry and jack pine. Next on the whitetails' selective browse menu are aspen, beaked hazel, paper birch, balsam fir and red pine.

As browse, the native red oak and beechnut found

Acorns are a prime food source wherever they are found.

here are low on the list of preferred food sources. However, in the fall acorns and beechnuts are highly prized by northern forest whitetails, and the deer feed heavily on them until they are completely consumed. Soft mast such as black cherries and hawthorn are also high on a whitetail's list of preferred foods, but are generally absent by the time the early bow seasons open.

Mast crop production in the region can be very inconsistent from one year to the next. It's not unusual for a bountiful year to be followed by one or two years of complete mast crop failure.

Central United States

This region includes all of what is usually referred to as the Midwest plus some northern portions of Alabama, Mississippi and Arkansas; the western half of Tennessee; most of the western two-thirds of Kentucky; and portions of eastern Oklahoma. The region includes two distinctly different types of whitetail habitat – the oak and hickory forests stretching across the southern tier of the region and the wide belt of heavy agriculture that runs northward to the southern Great Lakes.

While broken here and there by often sizeable areas of farming, much of the southern half of the central U.S. consists of rolling hardwood-covered ridges ranging in elevation from several hundred feet (in Mississippi) to several thousand feet (the Ouachita Mountains of Arkansas). These forests consist primarily of various oaks and usually

include a significant number of hickory trees.

As one might suspect, oak mast is a very important food source for whitetails all across this area. In some locations the deer may show a preference for red-oak acorns or pin-oak acorns, but the favored mast fruit throughout most of this area is the white-oak acorn. When these begin to fall each autumn, there's no better place to take a stand than along an oak-covered ridge top. Other whitetail-favored mast crops include beechnuts, sumac tops, persimmon and honey locust pods. When mast-crop foods are not ripe or available, deer in this region readily browse on native plants like common pokeberry, poison ivy, greenbrier, nettles, goldenrod, sumac and a tremendous variety of other forbs and herbs. And where present, agricultural crops such as soybeans, corn and hay also make up a significant part of their diet.

Across the upper Midwest, where there is much more farmland than wooded or brush-covered tracts, grain and hay crops tend to make up a large percentage of whitetails' annual diet. In fact, some studies show that corn, soybeans and hay crops can account for upwards of 70 percent of the food ingested. However, scattered all through this country you'll still find sizeable stands of hardwoods, and when the white-oak acorns begin to fall about the time of the first frost, deer leave every other food source to eat their fill of the sweet, meaty mast crop. In some areas, beechnuts and locust pods are also favored fall food sources.

At times of the year when mast is not available or when crop fields lay barren, upper-Midwestern whitetails will turn to a variety of grasses and browse. Favored food sources through late winter and spring include the new growth found on sassafras, ash, maple, elm and other native trees.

Harvesting grain fields makes deer more accessible to hunters.

Southeast

The terrain, foliage and climate of the region known as the Southeast varies so greatly from north to south and east to west that it would be virtually impossible to cover it as a single unit of whitetail habitat. Within this region are rugged eastern mountains topping 6,000 feet in elevation, highland plateaus covered by hardwood forests hundreds of square miles in size, pinelands intensely managed to produce fast growing soft-woods for lumber and paper products, vast agricultural areas, lowland coastal plains and swamps so densely grown with vegetation that a man cannot step off a beaten path or roadway. And all of it is home to the whitetail. What these deer prefer to eat varies just as much as the terrain and foliage found in every corner of this region.

Highland whitetails found in the predominately hardwood forests of the Appalachian Mountains enjoy a food base similar to that found in the southern tier of the Northeast region. Favored browse in the northern portion of this region, which extends up through most of Pennsylvania, includes sumac, sugar maple, sassafras, honeysuckle, hawthorn, greenbrier, poison ivy, crabapple, locust, aspen and ash. Favored mast crops include a variety of acorns, black cherries, beechnuts, and the fruits from hawthorn and crabapple.

On the southern end of the Appalachians, which extends into the upper third of northeastern Alabama, whitetails still selectively feed on many of these same food sources. However, where soft mast such as persimmons, apples and wild grapes are found, the deer feed heavily on these. The favored fall foods are still the acorn and beechnut.

White settlers first moved onto the Piedmont Plateau, which stretches from western Maryland to east-central Alabama, during the late 1700s. The region was wild then, with vast hardwood forests with only minimal natural openings. Whitetails were abundant and early farmers supplemented their meager crops by market-hunting deer for both meat and hides. Old records reveal that some 600,000 deer hides were shipped from Georgia alone between 1755 and 1773. However, by 1900 the expansive forests of the piedmont were all but gone, and so were the deer.

Extensive restocking programs began during the late 1930s and continued until the early 1960s. The region is once again home to a healthy population of whitetails, and more than half of the 63,000 square miles that make up the Piedmont

Plateau are again covered by mixed hardwood and pine forests. Japanese honeysuckle has become an extremely important and favored browse for the deer here, and whitetail experts claim they utilize it heavily year round. Other browse preferred by deer include sumac, greenbrier, poison ivy, dogwood, sassafras, tulip poplar and blackberry leaves. A wide range of oaks are found in this region. Deer feed heavily on the acorns from most oaks, but show a real preference for the white-oak acorn. Other hot mast crops to concentrate on during the hunting season include wild grape and honey locust. Whitetails will flock to a stand of honey locust trees to strip fallen pods of the beans inside.

One of the most varied whitetail habitats found in the United States is the coastal plain that begins in the southern tip of Texas and extends east to include Florida, then turns north all the way to New York. This lowland plain juts 600 miles up the Mississippi River to Cape Girardeau, Missouri. Along much of its length, the region extends inland for 200 to 400 miles.

In much of the southern portion of this region, quality whitetail habitat – or habitat that contains deer at all – is limited, and the overall number of deer relatively low. This is mainly due to the fact that the majority of the bottomland hardwoods that once made up much of this region have been cleared to make room for low-quality agricultural crop production. In many other areas hardwood forests have been practically eliminated to make room for commercial production of much faster growing soft pines, which offer little in the way of year-round food sources for sustaining a large number of deer.

Hunting opportunities in much of the coastal plain are limited. However, there are a few bright spots where deer numbers are high, even though deer size is on the small side. The Dismal Swamp area of coastal North Carolina is a prime example. Here deer are anything but scarce, thanks largely to the production of corn and soybean crops in areas surrounding the huge, uninhabited marshy tangle of cane, greenbrier and commercially grown pines.

Small stands of hardwoods still provide some mast crop for coastal whitetails, and as in other regions where the whietail is found, acorns from the various types of oak are important fall food sources that will attract deer. Other favored mast crops include beechnuts, ripe persimmons, honey locust, and where found, papaws. The variety of browse from north to south includes nearly 300 different types of plants. Some of the most widely found will be sassafras, greenbrier, mulberry, swamp cyrilla, Japanese honeysuckle, yaupon and poison ivy.

West

Western whitetails, which include those deer inhabiting the foothills of the Rocky Mountains and those that make the Great Plains home, are generally the most visible of all geographical whitetail populations. The reason why is simple – these deer inhabit a region with generally sparse cover. When it's feeding time, deer often must travel across open ground to reach food sources, which are commonly wide open river- or creek-bottom hay or crop fields. Unless deer remain bedded in a pocket of heavy cover or in a strip of thick brush along a western stream, they are usually out in the open.

During midwinter, deer in much of the northern Rocky Mountain West feed heavily on browse that often includes Douglas fir, western red cedar, cottonwood and quaking aspen. Other browse commonly fed upon by hungry whitetails includes ponderosa pine, snowberries, lichens and, where found, bearberry and myrtle.

Whitetails all through the non-coastal West tend to be more abundant in areas with some agricultural crop production. One of the best places to intercept a good mountain-valley buck is in or near a creek-bottom alfalfa field. In areas where corn is grown, whitetails will readily forage for crop remnants once the temperatures begin to drop and the snow begins to fly. Concentrate on these areas when hunting a late season.

Other Areas

The habitat types and geographical regions already covered account for the vast majority of whitetails in the United States, and the food sources detailed are among the most widely utilized. The following section looks at several smaller areas within the country where whitetails can be found. In a few of these areas deer are either totally protected or only limited hunting opportunities are available.

WEST TEXAS – The Edwards Plateau of west-central Texas is one of the best known whitetail-producing areas in the country. This area is often referred to as the "Hill Country" due to its rolling topography, which in most places is sparsely covered with a variety of short oaks, honey mesquite and ash juniper. Spanish oak, scrub oak, blackjack oak, post oak and live oak are the favored food sources for the deer, in the form of either browse

Western whitetails will often travel long distances across open terrain to feed in crop fields.

or the acorns produced by these trees. Other favorite mast foods include persimmon and honey mesquite. The ever present prickly pear cactus is also heavily consumed by deer here.

To the north of the Edward Plateau lie the rolling grass plains of north Texas. This natural prairie area is dotted with stands of various oaks and honey mesquite, providing browse and mast for a healthy whitetail population. The native woody plants and forbs utilized by deer include juniper, saltbush, nailwort, red berry and broomweed. North-central Texas whitetails also feed extensively on prickly pear cactus, accounting for as much as 50 percent of their diet in some areas.

The Trans-Pecos area of extreme western Texas is home to the lowest deer densities found in the state, and for good reason. This is extremely arid country with a limited amount of suitable cover and food sources for whitetails. Several small mountain ranges offer adequate habitat for deer, both whitetails and mule deer. At the higher elevations you'll find pinyon pine, ponderosa pine, juniper and some oaks, which provide food sources for the deer. In the majority of this desolate part of the state, rolling sandy or clay hills offer meager growths of grama grass, mesquite and yucca, which offer minor food sources for a very sparse whitetail population. However, find a good food source here and you've located a definite hot spot to hunt.

OREGON AND WASHINGTON – Whitetails are found in only a few isolated pockets in these two states, and hunting opportunities are extremely limited. Commonly referred to as Columbian whitetail deer, the majority of these deer can be found on two easily defined locations. One area is the Columbian White-tailed Deer National Wildlife Refuge, which straddles the Washington-Oregon border near the mouth of the Columbia River. The other area is found along the North Umpqua River near Roseburg, Oregon.

Like the whitetails found along the northern Rockies, the Columbian whitetail of the Pacific Northwest tends to frequent river- and creek-bottom hay fields, which surely provide a large percentage of their diet. And like their cousins 300 or 400 miles to the east, these deer likely also browse on many of the same woody plants and forbs where they are found.

FLORIDA KEYS – These tiny whitetails have not been legally hunted since the late 1930s and can be found on some of the islands known as the Florida Keys, southwest of Miami. The strongest population can be found on Big Pine Key, where

the Key Deer National Wildlife Refuge is located. The heaviest concentrations of these diminutive whitetails are found on those islands with some slash pine forest. When subjected to burns, these pine stands provide a variety of food for the deer. Among favored food sources are white indigo berry, saffron plum, Indian mulberry, brittle thatch palm and most anything else that grows on these small islands.

SOUTHERN ROCKIES – Across southern Arizona and New Mexico we find the small Coues' deer. A New Mexico game department study once described this subspecies of the whitetail as "too common to be considered rare and too rare to be considered common." The Coues' deer continues to be one of the least studied whitetails, but its numbers remain stable and hunting is allowed in most of its U.S. and Mexican ranges.

These deer are found in a wide range of habitat, from near-desert-like conditions to mountain growths of oak-pine forests. Most of these deer are found at elevations of 4,000 to 8,000 feet. The majority tend to prefer areas where relatively heavy oak and pine growths meet arid grasslands, indicating that these deer prefer a varied diet.

Like all whitetails, the Coues' variety will readily leave most other food sources to feed on acorns from fruit-bearing oaks in the fall, but most of their diet throughout the year consists of browse and native forbs. During the fall, fallen leaves become a significant food source, especially those from mountain mahogany. Other widely utilized browse include sumac, skunkbush and silktassel.

Opportunity Feeders

Whitetails, no matter where they are found, are selective feeders and will show definite preferences for certain food sources at certain times of the year. However, they are also opportunistic feeders, and when survival dictates, these remarkable animals can feed on just about any plant life. Whitetails are classified as ruminants, with a complex four-chambered stomach that allows them to digest and utilize foods that cannot be consumed by humans.

Where there is an abundance of high-quality food, whitetails will selectively choose plants or parts of plants with noticeable discrimination, choosing to dine first on those plants which best meet their nutritional needs. While whitetails are generally considered browsers, many whitetail experts point out that they are just as much grazers. Depending on what's the most palatable and digestible at the time, whitetails will readily switch from browse to a wide range of grasses. During the course of a full year, these deer will regularly feed on fruits, nuts, sedges, grasses, forbs and mushrooms, as well as trees and shrubs.

Supplemental Feeding

All across the country deer hunters and private land managers are now working to improve or support whitetail habitat with poor-quality food sources. These efforts include the widespread planting of food plots where the natural forage base is inadequate, or the use of feeders to provide a supplemental food source at times when the whitetails' needs are highest.

Much can be done to improve the deer-supporting capacity of any piece of property, whether it is 40 acres or 1,000 acres in size. To insure they have quality deer to hunt, landowners are now planting a tremendous variety of food sources to be

specifically left for deer and other wildlife. These include small cornfields, stands of soybeans, sizeable patches of clover or alfalfa, and even a number of new or nonnative plant types, some of which have been biologically engineered specifically for feeding deer. One such product is Mossy Oak's Biologic, a highly digestible, high-protein food source that was originally developed for deer-farming operations in New Zealand.

Game feeders come in all types, from simple gravity feeders that drop out grain or pellets as the deer continue to feed, to sophisticated motor-operated arrangements with timers that can be set to feed only at specific times. When used as an attractant for hunting deer, such feeders are commonly filled only with favored grain sources, such as corn or soybeans. However, where landowners are honestly attempting to improve the quality of the deer on their property, a growing number are now switching to mineral-enhanced high-protein pellets. They are mixed with corn to draw the deer to the superior food source. 🦌

Game feeders are popular for attracting deer in some areas.

FABULOUS FOOD PLOTS

by Carl Ganter

Tim Dugas and his 160-class "Oak Island" buck

Throughout much of the whitetail's range, a significant amount of harvested cropland undergoes a fall tillage process. To a hunter this is bad news because fields that once drew large numbers of deer, and probably some good bucks, suddenly go dead. Why? Simple – once the food is gone, the deer are gone. For this reason I spend a good amount of time in the spring and summer planning and planting food plots of the type that draw big bucks throughout the entire hunting season.

I do all of my hunting in Minnesota. As a bowhunter, I want food plots that draw deer early in the season (mid-September) until the end of the season (December 31). Several years ago, when my two hunting friends and I decided to experiment with food plots on my property, we didn't know what to plant. We tried corn for a couple of years, and that worked OK, but some years the crop failed and with it our hopes of having great late-season hunting. After doing a bit of research we decided to try the food-plot products made by a Minnesota company called Wildlife Buffet. Our reasoning was not scientific. In fact, we simply figured that if the company was from "Up North" their products must be designed to survive tough weather conditions.

First we went for a walk around my property (about 200 acres) and picked out spots where we'd love to have a food plot. You know the kind of spots – places far from roads and noisy backyards where a mature buck would feel comfortable during legal shooting light at any time of the year. My dream spot for a future food plot was on a small oak island in the middle of a wet swamp. I didn't know if it was possible to put one there, but hey, a guy can dream, can't he?

Because we were new to this game, we checked out the website for Wildlife Buffet (www.wildlifebuffet.com) for advice on how to

proceed. It didn't sound difficult, so we decided to go for it.

Our plan was to plant several small food plots throughout the property, including the oak island. We thought that the smaller plots would allow several doe/fawn families to have their own plot without a great deal of competition. In addition, it was our hope that once the rut kicked in, bucks would be forced into traveling from food plot to food plot to find receptive does. Such a situation would give my two hunting partners and me the opportunity to hunt at the same time without being on top of each other.

It was early June when we headed for the oak island. We started by applying Round-Up (a herbicide) to all the open areas of the island to kill the weeds. After about a week, we went back to the island carrying a small rototiller. Turning over the soil went better than expected, and in a few hours we had good soil for planting. With a high-protein perennial blend called Alpha Buck Spring in hand, we simply started broadcasting (a fancy word for throwing) seeds all over the newly turned-up earth. Once the seed was gone, we grabbed garden rakes and covered the seed with about an eighth-inch of dirt.

It took only 3 days for the plants to emerge from the soil. Since it looked like our efforts were going to pay off, we put up three treestands to handle different wind conditions and left the area alone for the rest of the spring and summer.

To say that a lot of deer, including big bucks, were drawn to the oak island would be an understatement. In fact, I was amazed at how all of our food plots attracted and held deer on my property. And while I'd like to conclude this story with an account of the huge buck that I shot off the oak island, I can't. For that, you'll have to talk to Tim, one of my hunting partners. Now the oak island is his dream spot!

Let Big Bucks Show You
Where They Are

by Toby Bridges

Wherever whitetails are found, during the course of their daily or seasonal activities, they leave behind telltale signs that give away their presence. Learning to read the sign and to understand exactly what you are looking at, why the deer created it and how to utilize this information to better locate your stand is the first step to becoming a good whitetail detective.

To the trained eye, even the smallest clue, such as the way a track imprints into the ground or how the tops of certain plants have been nibbled away, can have a significant meaning. Then there will be those times when an area is so torn up with rubs and scrapes that even the hunter with the poorest vision or lack of whitetail-hunting savvy will realize that here is a hunting hot spot. The following section looks at how to better interpret the sign you find.

Tracks

We will begin by taking a look at the most basic of deer sign, deer tracks. It stands to reason that where there are lots of deer, there ought to be lots of tracks. And if you're out to harvest just any deer, an abundance of tracks in a given area may be the only sign you need to consider. However, if you have your sights set on taking a buck of true trophy-class proportions, you need to know whether or not a good buck made any of those tracks.

How many times in the past has a hunting buddy pointed to a set of tracks in soft dirt or mud and commented that they were definitely made by a buck because the imprints of the dewclaws were visible? Truth is, both bucks and does, young and old, have dewclaws. In very soft soil or mud, the tracks of either will often show the dewclaws. On hard or very solid ground, neither bucks nor does will leave dewclaw imprints. However, in soil that is somewhere in between, the heavier weight of a big buck may cause the deer to sink deeper and to leave a deeper imprint, including the dewclaw. The tracks of lighter does and younger bucks may not push down far enough for the dewclaw to show.

There are more accurate indications that a specific track could have been left by a buck and not a doe. Length of a track is in itself not a definite indicator of the sex of the animal that left it. When looking at a big track with hoof marks that measure 3 to 4 inches in length and sink deeper into the ground than other tracks in the same soil, truthfully all you can determine is that it was left by a big deer. However, an old doe that reaches 5 or 6 years of age can also display a long track, and where there's plenty of forage through the year, some older does can reach nearly the weight of a 2 1/2-year-old buck.

This isn't to say that size cannot help determine whether a track was left by a good buck or by an overly large doe. The track of a big doe may match the length of a buck's track, but it is almost always much narrower. Once a whitetail buck reaches maturity at 3 1/2 to 4 1/2 years of age, his hooves can be nearly as wide as long, leaving a boxy imprint.

When a mature buck walks, the toes of the hoof tend to splay more than those of even the biggest doe. Also, the tracks of a doe can usually be distinguished by the placement of the rear footsteps. It is very common for a doe to set her rear feet down almost exactly where she placed her front feet. As often as not, the rear hoof marks will overstep to some degree the tracks of the front hooves. A buck places his rear feet down noticeably to the rear of his front feet. Older, more mature bucks also walk with hooves turned more outward.

Travel Routes

Whitetails establish very predictable routines, most of which involve travel from one spot to another for one reason or another. Where this travel is concentrated and possibly exercised on almost a daily basis, the deer will establish very distinct trails. In areas with less defined movement whitetails will often establish favored travel corridors that permit them to move from one location to another secretively or with less interaction with unfavorable obstacles or forces, such as human development or other intrusion into the whitetails' habitat.

Well-established trails can be extremely easy to locate since many are literally beaten-down paths leading through a weedy field, along the edge of a standing cornfield, down from a ridge point, to or from a favorite feeding area, along a heavily wooded fencerow, or wherever the deer travel regularly. One of the best ways to find a well-used trail is to walk down a dry creek bed or a shallow waterway. Creek crossings can be extremely visible, and where deer have been using the same crossings for years, they will commonly cut a deep notch or groove into the bank. Another location where deer travel often becomes very concentrated is around the upper end of a cove on a lake, around a marsh or on the upper end of a large pond.

Travel corridors can be wider, and the deer using them may not move along the exact same route any two times they pass through. Because of that travel pattern, locating even a well-used travel corridor can be more difficult due to the seeming lack of tracks. A deer that walks along a given route just once or twice a week may not disturb natural ground cover enough to be noticeable, especially if that deer passes through 20 or so yards from the exact route it traveled previously.

Look for these corridors where a narrow strip of timber separates two fields, along natural shelves that can offer easier walking on an otherwise steep incline, or along valley bottoms running between ridges or extremely heavy cover. While does, fawns and yearling bucks will readily head out into the open, mature trophy-class bucks may be more secretive where you hunt. These are the deer that use travel corridors the most. And these bucks know other bucks are likely to use these same out-of-sight passageways, so look for territorial rubs and scrapes that are definite signs that a buck or two uses a corridor. Tracks in snow always make it

SCRAPE HUNTING

by John Sloan

John Sloan with a beautiful Illinois buck

Let me say right up front that I don't place a lot of faith in hunting over a scrape. Now, this may go against everything you've heard or read, but in my book, devoting an excessive amount of time to hunting a single scrape is more often than not a waste of that time.

Keep in mind that a mature whitetail buck may have as many as 50 to 60 active scrapes during the pre-rut. That's a lot of scrapes to check, even on a semi-daily basis. And the chances of being in the right stand over the right scrape when a buck does check it can be slim at best. This is especially true when you consider the fact that most scrape checking is done at night.

Still, scrape hunting can be very productive. I have killed some nice bucks by hunting over or near scrapes, although most were not record-book bucks. Through my time spent scrape hunting, I have realized a few key elements that can improve the odds while hunting them, and they are not hard to understand or recognize.

Let me start with the right scrape to hunt. I key in on two scrape locations. The first is what many writers incorrectly call a boundary scrape because they think it defines a buck's boundary, which is pure meadow muffin! A boundary scrape is simply on the boundary of something – terrain or structure.

I pay the most attention to late-appearing boundary scrapes on the edges of fields, fence lines, and streams. Now, when I refer to a late-appearing scrape, I mean one that appears after the first little bloom of scraping activity.

My favorite boundary scrapes appear in a tree line on the edge of a grown-up field. They have several positive factors: adjacency to a probable bedding area, cover on both sides and high travel probabilities.

The second place I look for scrapes is in really thick cover. It has been my experience that these scrapes usually are made by larger bucks. It has also been my experience that these scrapes almost always are scent checked by the buck from a distance. These are difficult scrapes to hunt with a bow, but it can be done.

These two kinds of scrapes are usually made by truly wise, cautious, mature bucks. When you spot one of these scrapes, look it over with your binoculars from a distance. If you decide to hunt it, be prepared to hunt it right then. Where do you hunt it from? You hunt it from the same place the buck stops to check it. That place may be as much as 75 yards away – downwind.

Hunting scrapes can be a real challenge. But take the time to find those scrapes that bucks will visit during shooting hours and you have yourself a true hot spot.

easier to find these hidden travel routes, so never miss the opportunity to get out and scout right after a relatively fresh snowfall.

A rifle hunter can easily cover most travel corridors of 100 to 150 yards across, while the bowhunter may have to look for areas where deer travel becomes more concentrated. Look for a bottleneck that cuts the width of the corridor, or a place where a bend in a creek bed, a ridge point or a deep gully restricts deer movement. Whitetails will readily move around these obstacles and continue on through the corridor. Where travel becomes more predictable is the place to hang a bowhunting stand.

Beds

A buck that tops 250 or 300 pounds on the hoof will definitely leave a much larger bed depression than a buck of smaller stature or a doe. And unless a big buck is traveling with a doe in estrus, during the active pre-rut and the rut itself, the deer is usually a loner. So, when you locate a large depression that's all by itself, you are more than likely in the bedding area of a good buck.

If you hunt in an area with wooded ridges, look for buck bedding sites just below the crest of a ridge. From these locations the deer can spot danger approaching from below and is only a few leaps from safety down one side of the ridge or back across to the other side should a hunter approach from nearly any direction. In farm country, check out pockets of heavy grass and weeds that are surrounded by farm fields, while a slight rise in a marshy location may offer the dry bedding a buck may seek. Deer can and will bed just about anywhere, but most of the time you'll find them bedded in cover that offers protection, seclusion and an avenue of escape, whether it's a several-acre honeysuckle thicket or small patch of blackberry briar.

Droppings

Adult whitetails spend more time on feeding than any other single activity. They are selective feeders, but even when they are traveling to preferred food sources, they will stop periodically to take a few bites of various browse, mast crops or grasses. This steady ingestion of food while on the move means that you are likely to encounter droppings just about anywhere.

Big deer will leave behind large droppings. When you locate a high concentration of deer droppings, it usually indicates that you've located a heavily used feeding area. And where there are lots of droppings of various sizes from small to large, the sign generally indicates use by does and fawns. However, when you find large scattered or isolated pellets, chances are they came from a mature buck.

Buck Rubs

Easily the most identifiable buck sign a hunter will encounter is the buck rub. Many highly educated and experienced whitetail biologists and professional game managers claim that the true meaning or purpose of rubs has never been positively identified. But for the trophy-buck hunter, these scarred-up trees and saplings are the calling cards that tell us a good buck lives in this neighborhood.

For decades, hunters felt the first buck rubs of the year, which usually begin to show up in late September or early October, were made to facilitate rubbing away the drying velvet from new antler growth. However, we now know that this thin membrane will dry and peel away from the hardened antler beneath whether a buck rubs or not. Likewise, most hunters have long believed that the early rubs found on small finger-diameter saplings were the work of young 1½-year-old bucks. Not anymore. Now many very knowledgeable trophy-buck hunters realize that big bucks also make a large number of these small rubs. However, when you find a 10- or 12-inch tree that has been whittled down to half its original size, you know immediately that it was done by a massive set of antlers sitting atop a powerful neck. In other words, big deer can and will make small rubs, but only big deer can make the truly big rubs.

The most widely accepted reason for rubs is that they are a means of communication. And many very experienced whitetail hunters have concluded that rubs in different locations at different times of the season can have a totally different meaning. For instance, early rubs may just be made by a dominant buck venting a little frustration, or a young buck with its first true antler growth testing the new headgear. And where you find clusters of rubs, they are usually the work of more than a single buck, maybe a bachelor group of bucks attempting to impress one another.

Then there's what are often referred to as signpost rubs. These are the rubs most hunters scout so hard to find. It is believed that bucks make a series of these to mark travel routes. The rubbed area of the trunk is often found on only one side of each tree, indicating the direction in which the buck was traveling when the rub was made – and likely the direction the buck will be headed when following the route at a later date. When these rubs are found on larger-diameter trees, they also serve as territorial markers, forewarning any other buck that happens to trespass into the area.

While the size and severity of a rub serves as a warning to other bucks, a rub also informs breeding does that there is a dominant buck in the area. In addition to demonstrating the buck's prowess with his antlers and his inherent strength, a rub also allows the buck to deposit scent from its forehead gland, which further warns other bucks of his dominance and makes does aware of his claims to the territory. It's not unusual to observe a doe nosing a rub to more closely identify the scent. Does have even been seen licking a buck rub.

Scrapes

Bucks also commonly rake away leaves or other ground cover with their hooves or antlers, then urinate on the barren ground to establish another sign of communication – the scrape. And like rubs, scrapes can vary greatly in size, from the size of a small saucer to an area the size of your living room! Again like rubs, scrapes are believed to serve as warnings of dominance by mature bucks to subordinate bucks. Scrapes also communicate to does that a buck is ready to breed. The doe that deposits her scent by urinating in a scrape in turn lets a buck know that she is receptive to breeding.

Scrapes may be found just about anywhere a buck travels, but since they are tools of communication, deer tend to make them where other deer are most likely to encounter them. Look for scrapes along the edges of fields, especially where an overhanging low branch will allow a buck to leave additional scent with its forehead glands or by licking and chewing on the tips of the limb. Other excellent places to find a scrape are along an old woods road (particularly one that follows along the spine of a ridge), near heavily used trails and along known travel corridors.

When approaching a suspected scrape location from downwind, you'll often smell a heavily used scrape before seeing it. Sometimes two or three bucks may use the same scrape, and can deposit a lot of strong urine when trying to get the attention of does approaching estrus.

When looking for a good stand site near a scrape, keep in mind that bucks very often wind- or scent-check scrapes, meaning they don't actually walk

Scrapes are found under an overhanging branch.

right up and poke their nose into the spot of uncovered earth. Instead, they approach the scrape from downwind, often getting no closer than 50 yards or so from the scrape. If they pick up the scent of a doe that's used the scrape, they may move in to investigate closer. However, if you have your stand within bow range of an active scrape and the buck comes in from downwind to check for the scent of recent activity, chances are the only scent he will pick up on will be yours.

LOOK FOR POST-SEASON SIGN

by Jay Gregory

I do very little scouting once the seasons begin. In fact, the majority of my scouting for the next bowhunting season is done very, very early in the year, like in February and March. This is a great time of the year to see things you'll never see early in the fall when there are still lots of leaves on the trees. In late winter everything is barren and everything the deer have been doing for months is very visible.

Jay Gregory with a Kansas trophy that scored 168 B&C points

Major trails and travel corridors stick out like a sore thumb, and other sign like rubs and old scrapes are more easily located. I know from experience that come next fall the deer will be following the same movement patterns, and if I were to venture into the area at the end of October or early November, I would find rubs, scrapes and well-used travel routes in exactly the same areas.

In fact, I have so much confidence in the deer following the same well-established patterns that I hang the majority of my stands for the next hunting season, which is still 6 or 7 months away, during this time of the year. One thing is for certain – by hanging stands this early, I give those wary old bucks plenty of time to forget about any commotion I've made while getting stands in place and cutting shooting lanes.

With the complete lack of foliage to block anything from sight, I also spend a great deal of time searching for the best ways into and out of a stand site. Experience has taught me that a hunter usually has his best opportunity at a mature 4- to 6-year-old record-book-class whitetail buck the very first time a stand is hunted. So no matter how good a stand location may be, I'll stay out of that stand until the timing of the pre-rut or rut and the wind is absolutely perfect for hunting that stand. I don't want to blow my chances at a super buck by taking the wrong route to the stand.

Actually, I feel that most stand locations are given away by hunters as they leave an area at the end of an evening hunt. This is when deer are most likely present, and a hunter trying to ease down from his stand and back out of the woods runs the greatest chances of being spotted or winded by the deer. And once a season-wise old buck knows you're in his domain, he more than likely will move to another area.

That is the reason why I do very little pre-season and in-season scouting. I don't want to intrude into these areas where the buck or bucks I'm hunting live. I want them to stay right where they are until every condition is perfect for hunting them. Most hunters ruin any chances they have at such bucks by spending far too much time scouting in the areas they plan to hunt.

The shed antlers and huge tracks I find during my post-season winter scouting tells me of the bucks that made it through the season and through the winter. And once I know there is a quality buck in an area, I'll spend quite a bit of time through the summer watching deer feeding out in the fields. I'm a firm believer in using cam-trackers placed along trails leading in and out of these areas to get a good look at a buck I may hunt that coming fall. If I can get a visual on one of these bucks come early October, I know I've found a buck that will be in the area I'll hunt come November.

When it's time to hunt, I don't trespass into the area I will be hunting. I don't go looking for rubs and scrapes. These things don't mean all that much to me. Trouble is, once a hunter finds these things, chances are he's already bumped that buck out of the area. Rattling is the tactic I use most to produce the quality bucks I hunt. And with my stands already hung in areas I know big bucks frequent, all I have to do is get in and out of the woods without letting them know I'm there. And that can be challenging enough.

TECHNIQUES FOR RECORD-BOOK BUCKS

Set Up in the Right Spot

with Mark Drury

Taking a big, mature whitetail buck on his own home turf more often than not requires a considerable investment in time and effort to determine his daily travel routine. And even once that has been established there is still that element of luck – being in the right place at the right time! No one seems to be better at it than M.A.D. game-call maker and hunting-video producer Mark Drury of Missouri.

"Oh, I believe in luck," says Drury with a smile, "but I also know that any hunter looking to hang his tag on a really good buck – especially a particular book-class buck – must work at being lucky. Knowing exactly where to locate a stand and when to be in that stand are two factors that can swing luck in a hunter's favor."

Besides looking for obvious sign in the way of big tracks, rubs, scrapes and other telltale evidence that a big buck lives in an area, Drury also concentrates heavily on land features and travel corridors that can naturally put a season-wise old buck in his sights. And Mark doesn't wait until it's time to get out hunting before putting his stands in place. This savvy hunter, who takes full advantage of the archery, muzzleloader and modern gun seasons, spends many hours sitting in what he likes to refer to as observation stands doing just that – observing the deer in his hunt areas.

"My brother Terry and I hang these observation stands and really watch and study the deer early in the fall. When you spot a mature buck in an area over and over, for days or weeks, you start to piece together the edges . . . the points . . . and the funnels he is using," states Drury.

He goes on to say, "A lot of people look for classic funnels, like strips of timber or creek bottoms that connect fields and thickets. But I also look for something as subtle as a slight depression or saddle in a ridge or a point off a hogback ridge – any little feature that might funnel does and a big buck. Then I hang a treestand nearby, getting the wind right and taking into consideration food sources, bedding thickets, and things like that."

Whitetails are opportunists, and when faced with an obstacle that requires an effort to cross or pass through, they will very often follow the path of least resistance and go around or skirt such obstacles. For instance, say a sizeable plum thicket forms a nearly impenetrable wall along the edge of an agricultural field. During daylight hours does may walk along the field side of the thicket, in plain view, without much reservation. However, a buck of trophy-class proportions will likely tend to be a little more secretive and choose to travel down the back side of such a thicket, out of sight. And here is the most likely spot to hang a stand, not along the field edge.

Another situation where buck travel is often naturally funneled is where a cove from a nearby lake juts back into the timber or heavy cover, or around the upper end of a small farm pond or lake, or around a swamp or marshy area. Whitetails are excellent swimmers, but the vast majority of times will avoid getting soaked and will travel around these features. Many times you'll find a heavily used trail where the majority of this traffic is funneled around the point of water. However, don't give up on such a location if you don't find a distinct trail. Look for scattered tracks that may indicate the spot is still a well-used travel corridor, one that's maybe 25 to 50 yards back from the water.

Mark knows that the corners of a field can also concentrate deer movement and hunts them regularly. Where corn is still standing in the field, the edge between the woods or heavy cover and the unharvested crop can be a great place to ambush a good buck that's on the prowl. But once the corn has been picked and the protective cover has been removed, or in places where a shorter crop such as soybeans was planted, heavy-horned bucks very often travel just far enough back into the heavy cover to be able to now and then look out into the open field. This travel corridor may be 20 to 50 yards back from the field's edge. However, where the field comes to a distinct corner, whitetail movement often becomes concentrated closer to the edge, and such locations can be a productive spot to hang a stand.

When hunting near the edge of a crop field where the deer feed on a regular basis, always keep in mind that big mature bucks are usually the last deer to work out into the open at dusk, and among the first to leave at dawn. Mark points out that to intercept these deer, you may find it necessary to move back away from the field. Look for buck sign that can tell you the spot may be a staging area, where a good buck lingers in the evening before slipping out to join does already in the field, or where he may wait to be joined by others in the first light of morning.

Like so many other consistently successful big-buck hunters, Drury is a firm believer in staying out of a stand if the wind direction isn't right. More often than he cares to admit, he will hang a stand in an extremely promising spot only to be kept from hunting that stand by wind direction that's all wrong for the location. Mark will be the first to share that one of the biggest mistakes a hunter can make is to continue to hunt a location when the wind currents are all wrong.

To avoid missing out on the opportunity to hunt a good buck in a particular area, Drury will usually take the time to scout for a secondary stand location. Often this stand site, which may be only a few hundred yards from the primary stand location, may be nearly as good as his first choice and will allow him to hunt the general area when the wind direction prevents him from hunting the primary location.

He points out that special care should always be taken when walking into a stand location, especially during a bowhunt. This seasoned archer is a firm believer in wearing calf-high rubber boots to keep from leaving a scent trail every time he walks into a stand site. In the same light, Drury also avoids making bare-hands contact with foliage, fences, tree trunks or anything else in his hunting area. Human scent can remain in an area for a day or longer after you've left, still alerting deer that a human has invaded their home. Also, never approach your stand location through or upwind of cover where you know deer may be bedded or feeding. Air currents will carry your scent to the deer and alert them to your presence.

Just how high a hunter places his stand can be something of a personal choice. Experienced bowhunters like Drury tend to agree that somewhere around 20 feet is a good height. Keep in mind that stands just 10 to 12 feet off the ground place the hunter so low that approaching deer can more easily spot the slightest movement, or detect a shape that's not natural.

The higher a hunter positions his stand, the less likely it is that a deer passing slightly downwind will pick up on human odor. Scent-carrying air currents drop back to earth farther away from a stand that's positioned 20 feet up than from a stand that's just half that height. Another advantage of a higher platform is that it gives the hunter a better view of the area and allows better detection of movement farther away. And the earlier a hunter realizes a buck is headed his way, the sooner he can ready bow or gun, or make the decision to rattle the horns or blow a grunt call.

High stands do have a downside. Keep in mind that the higher the stand is placed, the more difficult shot placement will be. This is especially true when trying to precisely place a broadhead-tipped arrow squarely through the vitals. The higher you get, the narrower the target below and the more you have to concentrate on the angle of the hit in order for the shot to create the needed trauma to heart, lungs and other vital organs for a clean, quick harvest of the buck.

Drury shares, "Right-handed archers will want to position their stand so the deer will most likely pass slightly to the hunter's left, while southpaw shooters will want the reverse, with the deer passing to their right. If you shoot a bow primarily from the sitting position, you'll find it next to impossible to pull your bow to full draw, take aim and shoot at anything that's directly in front of you. However, if you like to get to your feet and shoot from the standing position, exact stand position in relation to most deer movement isn't as critical. Still, the right-handed shooter, whether hunting with bow, muzzleloader or modern gun, who finds himself in a stand that's better suited for a left-handed hunter will feel awkward, and vice versa."

Whenever hunting from a treestand, safety should always be first and foremost in your mind. Drury says to always check out your stands well before the season to make sure that they are sound, that the chains or straps used to attach them are not damaged and to tighten loose bolts or replace those that are rusted or worn. He also points out that the wise hunter will never hang a treestand or hunt from one without wearing the proper safety belt or harness.

More good whitetail bucks are taken from well-located treestands than by any other tactic. There is more to putting yourself in the right place at the right time than simply sticking any stand in any tree. In the following pages of this chapter we will take a look at the variety of stands presently available to help you decide which is best for your style of hunting or the terrain and woods where you hunt, the various methods for getting from the ground and into the lofty platform, accessories that could up your chances for success, and more on hot stand locations.

Which Stand Is Right for Your Hunting?

Easily 80 percent of the whitetails I've taken over the years have been shot from an elevated stand of some sort, and at least another 10 percent were taken from a ground stand. Whether or not you enjoy those long waits for a good buck to show up, hunting from a strategically located stand site annually produces more good bucks from coast to coast than all of the other methods combined.

Properly situated and properly hunted, a good stand allows the hunter to take shots at deer that should have absolutely no idea that the hunter is there. And making a good hit on a target that's moving along calmly, or standing perfectly still, is a lot easier than making exact shot placement on a whitetail that's running and jumping wildly. This is especially true if you're bowhunting, where your target must generally be within 30 yards. Hunters have discovered that getting a shot at a relaxed buck is most easily accomplished from a stand positioned 15 to 25 feet off the ground.

Dozens of manufacturers now cater to the whitetail hunter's need to get off the ground, and today there is a tremendous variety of treestands to choose from. These basically fall into three different categories – fixed-position, climbing and ladder-type stands. Choosing the right type for your hunting needs can be nearly as important as having it in the right place. Here is a look at the different types of stands available and tips to choosing the right stand for your hunting.

Fixed-Position Stands

Touted as the most versatile type of all the portable treestands available, the fixed-position stand is also commonly the lowest priced of the commercially produced stands, due to simplicity of its design. Most consist of a standing platform, a small seat, support cables for the platform and either a chain or heavy nylon strap for attaching the stand to a tree. The average weight of this type stand will range from around 8 pounds on the light side up to 14 or 15 pounds on the heavy side, with the size of the standing platform in direct correlation to the weight. Generally speaking, the bigger the stand, the more it weighs.

The advantage of a fixed-position stand is that it can usually be hung on just about any tree. There are now even models that allow the stand to be hung level on a tree trunk that has considerable lean in one direction or another, which could be important in positioning the stand exactly where it needs to go. Bowhunters really tend to prefer stands of this type since they must be able to get as close as possible to the travel route of the buck they're after. Plus the simple construction of this type of stand usually keeps support braces or cables from interfering with the lower limb of the

Lone Wolf fixed-position treestand

bow, even if the bow is pulled to full draw from the sitting position.

One disadvantage of a fixed-position chain-on or strap-on stand is that the hunter must also pack in steps or a ladder arrangement for getting into the elevated stand, or getting it up there in the first place.

Personally, I look for trees with lots of limbs. One or two steps near the bottom often gets me to the first limb, and then I can go from limb to limb until I reach the stand. A few limbs also help break up my outline. A word of caution though – when using limbs to get to your stand, just make sure they are live limbs and are strong enough to support your weight. Also, be very careful during wet weather when limbs can become very slippery.

Climbing Stands

Stands of this type are often referred to as "self-climbers," but in reality are anything but self climbing. To operate one does require some effort and agility from the hunter, but in the right situations stands of this type can offer mobility lacking in other stand types.

As a rule, most climbing stands consist of two major parts – a standing platform and a separate seat that doubles as the climbing support. With

Lone Wolf climbing treestand

some designs the hunter actually sits in the seat (facing the tree) while climbing, while others require the hunter to stand on the lower platform and grasp onto the frame of the climbing seat. With either design, the hunter's feet usually slip into webbed straps attached to the top of the standing platform.

The actual climbing is accomplished by supporting your weight on the upper portion of the stand, either sitting in it or grasping it with your hands and supporting yourself with your arms, then lifting the lower platform with your legs. The standing platform is then repositioned (with your feet) on the tree trunk, allowing you to stand once again. The upper portion is then repositioned a foot or so higher on the trunk and the process repeated over and over until you've reached the height you intend to hunt, or a major limb prevents you from climbing any higher. The "inch-worm" process allows most climbing-stand users to reach 15 to 25 feet in just a few minutes.

Where there are lots of straight trees without any limbs on the lower 20- to 25-foot length of the trunk, climbing stands tend to be very popular. One advantage of this type of stand is that the user does not have to rely on screw-in (or strap-on) steps or a separate climbing ladder to get into the stand. Another advantage is that a hunter can quickly move locations with minimal disturbance to get closer to an observed movement pattern. And when positioned on a very straight tree trunk, a climbing stand can be easily moved around to offer the best possible shot angle. The main disadvantage is that many such stands weigh 20 to 30 pounds and can be quite a load to pack in to a distant stand site.

Some climbers have been designed specifically for hunting with a gun, positioning the hunter so he or she faces the tree, which does make a fine rest for those longer shots. However, a growing number of climbing-stand models now allow the hunter to face the tree or face away from the trunk, making them practical for the bowhunter who needs plenty of room for the lower limb of his bow when attempting a shot.

Ladder Stands

Without a doubt the easiest of all portable stands to put into position, and the easiest to climb in and out of – in the daylight or in the dark – is the ladder stand. However, convenience always comes with a price tag, and with ladder-type stands that price is bulk and weight. Many of these stands weigh 70 to 100 pounds.

While easy to set up, getting some of the heavier stands of this type into a semi-remote stand site often requires several people. For that reason, ladder stands tend to be more popular when used on privately owned lands, where they are often left in the same spot for the entire season. Once securely fastened to a tree, a good ladder stand can be extremely solid and a cinch to get in and out of, even without the aid of a flashlight in the pre-dawn darkness.

Most commercially produced ladder stands come with a number of 3- to 5-foot ladder sections that lock together, extending the sitting or standing platform 10 to 15 feet up against the tree. Some of the more comfortable models feature a standing platform and a padded seat and backrest.

One drawback to using a ladder-type stand is that the stand presents a very noticeable silhouette against the tree, especially the lower height models that position the hunter down around 10 feet. One solution is to cut small saplings and attach these to the legs of the ladder to break up the straight outline.

Permanent/Wooden Stands

In more than 35 years of whitetail hunting, I've had the opportunity to hunt from a great variety of not-so-portable stands. Most of these have been simple wooden platforms, either built from commercial lumber or the trunks of larger saplings, nailed to the trunks of two, three or four larger trees. Some have been big and roomy, others little more than a 2- or 3-foot section of two-by-eight positioned in the crotch of a tree. Then there have been those fully enclosed permanent stands that featured nearly all the comforts of a Holiday Inn, including a heater and sliding windows to shoot from. One even featured a mini library to make those long waits for a buck to show in the adjacent food plot more enlightening.

Even if you're hunting from a homemade platform you've built yourself, always check it for wood rot,

loose boards, rusted nails or anything else that could make the stand dangerous and unpredictable. Be especially sure to check the soundness of a homemade wooden ladder or wooden steps nailed directly to the tree or trees.

Tripod Stands

There are going to be those situations and habitats where it's impossible to even find a tree that's large enough for hanging an elevated portable stand, let alone one that's right where it needs to be. Much of south Texas offers very few trees large enough to accommodate a treestand. For years hunters here

have found portable tripod stands ideal for getting up and above much of the lower brush for a better view of their hunting area. Now hunters in many other regions of the country are utilizing tripod arrangements to hunt semi-open and low-brush whitetail habitat.

Unfortunately, tripod stands are big, bulky and heavy. Getting one to a stand site often requires the use of a four-wheel-drive pickup, a farm tractor or an ATV with a small trailer. The stands can usually be assembled and erected in less than an hour, but due to their size they really stand out. The legs can be brushed in to make them less conspicuous, and many hunters try to set them back in thick cover, a stand of cedars or other foliage to hide them. While tripod stands are usually far less than ideal for bowhunting, it's been done. However, since most feature a shooting rail of sorts, they can prove to be one of the best stands for the long-range rifleman.

Ground Stands/Blinds

As well as elevated stands work, there are some hunters who will never leave good old solid ground. And there is absolutely nothing wrong with a good ground stand or blind, provided it offers good shooting lanes, is reasonably concealed and is downwind of the deer. While it's tough, some hunters have even learned to successfully bowhunt from a ground-level blind.

Some of the best ground-level gun stands I've ever hunted from were old bulldoze piles near the edge of a field heavily fed on by deer. Not only will the pile of rotting tree trunks and limbs provide cover for the hunter, one can also prove to be a great rifle rest for taking those long shots.

A small amount of brush piled out away from the trunk of a big tree can also provide enough cover to prevent being spotted by passing deer. A number of hunting equipment suppliers now also offer a variety of camouflaged blinds. Some are as simple as a strip of camouflaged netting or cloth supported by fiberglass poles that can be easily pushed into the ground. Other commercially produced blinds are fully enclosed tent-like arrangements with a zippered door and windows or shooting ports.

Treestand Accessories

How you accessorize your deer-hunting stand will depend largely on the type of stand you'll be hunting from or the type of hunting you'll be doing. If you elect to go with a self-climbing stand, you won't have much use for a set of tree steps, and if you plan to hunt from a ground stand or blind, a safety strap or harness is unnecessary. Likewise, the bowhunter may have different needs than the gun or muzzleloader deer hunter.

The following is a look at those accessories that many of the whitetail hunting experts featured in this book deem as "necessities." When choosing the gear you will be taking into the stand with you, just keep in mind that more is not always better. Someone has to pack all of that stuff into and out of the deer woods, and that someone will likely be you.

Climbing Aids

Getting from the ground up to a strap-on or chain-on fixed-position stand 20 feet up in a big oak easily, quietly and safely is the first require-

Mark Drury with a record-book 8-pointer

ment of the hunter who chooses to hunt from that type of treestand. And most of us do – this is the number-one-selling type of stand. To get the job done, you may even consider using a set of climbing spikes, like those used by linemen to climb telephone or power poles. However, on public lands you could be in violation of the law for damaging trees, and if you skin up enough valuable oaks on private land, it's not likely that a landowner will invite you back. Here are a couple of alternatives.

LADDERS AND CLIMBING POLES – These come in several styles. Some feature sections that slip together to form a single ladder or climbing pole, and others allow the sections to be attached to the tree individually. The latter style gives the hunter more flexibility in the straightness of the tree being hunted. Short 4-foot sections can be strapped intermittently along the trunk of a crooked tree, while a 12-foot, 14-foot or 16-foot ladder or pole (made up of sections that slip together) will require a pretty straight tree.

Whether your ladder or climbing pole is made of interlocking or individual sections, these arrangements generally all attach to the tree in a similar manner. Practically all feature a rope or strap securely fastened to one side of the ladder or pole that goes around the backside of the trunk and is then pulled tight and either cinched, tied or buckled to the other side of the ladder or pole section. Ladder arrangements and climbing poles can be set up quickly and easily, and for that reason have been gaining in popularity. The one disadvantage is that enough sections to get a hunter 15 or so feet off the ground can easily weigh much more than the treestand.

TREE STEPS – The lightweight route to climbing a tree is the use of individual screw-in or strap-on steps. Depending on the type chosen, 10 to 12 of these will add only 2 or 3 pounds to the load being carried. Screw-in steps come in two types – as a one-piece unit or as a folding step that is more convenient to carry.

When using steps of the screw-in type, always make sure that the step is turned all the way in slightly past where the threads end. The one-piece screw-in steps often have a little flex, especially when supporting the weight of a big hunter, and the closer the step is to the tree the less likely it is to flex enough to allow the foot to slip off the end. Also keep in mind that the larger the step, the easier it will be to find with your foot when climbing that tree in pre-dawn darkness or when climbing down in the evening.

Screw-in steps can be difficult to get started into hardwoods such as oak or hickory, but there are several different tools that can be used to help give the pointed, threaded end of the step a bite into the tough wood. On some trees a heavy bark cover can make step installation difficult, and you may have to use a small belt axe to knock the bark free where you want the step.

Some hunters and landowners claim that screw-in steps damage the tree, and on many federal or state lands screw-in steps are prohibited. However, studies have revealed that the hole created by the threaded shank of a screw-in step is shallow, heals quickly and does little if any real harm to the tree. However, where landowners or regulations prohibit screw-in steps, strap-on arrangements work just fine and can be a lot easier to install. Whether you choose to use screw-in or strap-on steps, just be sure to place the steps close enough together to keep from having to stretch unnaturally to reach the next step.

Safety Belt or Harness

The number-one cause of accidents and fatalities during the annual deer seasons has absolutely nothing to do with mistaking another hunter for a deer or accidental discharge of a firearm. The number-one cause of accidents and fatalities during deer season is hunters falling from elevated treestands.

The vast majority of these accidents could be easily avoided if only those hunters would wear a safety belt or harness. Many treestand makers now ship a simple nylon web safety belt with every stand. When using this type of safety system, attach the belt to the tree at about head height when you are standing. Then put the belt around your body just under your armpits. If you happened to slip and fall, the belt would be high enough on your body to prevent you from turning upside down or sideways. A belt that rides down around your waist could cause injuries to internal organs if it suddenly cinched tight when stopping the weight of your fall.

Many top deer-hunting experts now rely on a more efficient safety harness, designed much like the harness arrangement found on parachutes. These harnesses are a lot more forgiving on the body should you fall, and will keep you upright. The better designs are also a lot more comfortable to wear and are less likely to get in the way when it's time to make those last-minute moves in the stand in order to get a shot.

Other Accessories

PULL-UP ROPE OR STRAP – Not only do you have to get yourself into the stand, but you also have to get your bow or gun and other gear up there as well – and back down at the end of the morning or evening hunt. Avoid using line that's smaller than 5/16-inch diameter. That scoped rifle can weigh 10 pounds or more, and thinner lines can easily be cut if caught on a sharp object. They are also more difficult to control when lowering things. The olive-drab green parachute cord that can be purchased at most army surplus stores makes a great pull-up rope. A few deer-hunting equipment suppliers also offer half-inch-wide straps with snaps at each end that are great.

SMALL SAW AND PRUNING SHEARS – No matter how perfect a stand may seem at first, there are always a few saplings and branches in the way, especially if you're bowhunting. A light, compact folding saw and set of pruning shears store easily and are worth their weight in gold.

BOW OR GUN HOLDER – Like other stand accessories, these also come in several varieties. One type attaches to the stand, another screws into the tree. (Some hunters use a spare screw-in step in place of the latter type.) Bow or gun holders keep the hands free for calling or rattling . . . or enjoying all those mid-morning or midday snacks you carried in with you.

FLAGGING OR TRAIL MARKERS – Finding your stand in broad daylight may be a cinch, but what about in the dark? A series of short sections of bright fluorescent orange flagging hung from low branches can mark the way. For finding the stand in pitch dark, many hunters now rely on reflective trail markers or pins that shine brightly when hit with the beam of a small flashlight.

SMALL FLASHLIGHT OR HEADLAMP – Getting in and out of the woods in the dark will require a light of some sort. Many hunters rely on the small "pen light" types that slip easily into a pocket so they'll rarely be forgotten in one's haste to get into the deer woods. However, many hunters are now opting for a light headlamp that leaves hands free for climbing in and out of the stand in the dark.

DAYPACK – To carry all of this gear, plus snack foods, maps, a hunting knife, a compass, personal relief items such as a pee bottle and toilet paper, or whatever else you feel is necessary for a successful and comfortable hunt, you'll need a good daypack. A cellular phone can be a lifesaver in an emergency, but remember: Deer hunting is suppose to be a one-on-one experience – just you and the deer. Turn off the phone before you put it in your day-pack and leave it off.

When to Place and Hunt Stands

Many knowledgeable whitetail hunters feel strongly that the best time to hunt a new stand is when that stand is first positioned. After that, they feel that wary trophy-class bucks quickly tune in on the fact that something isn't quite right, or begin to pick up on the human intrusion. Most successful big-buck hunters also believe that the more a stand site is hunted, the less productive it becomes. In other words, the deer begin to pattern the hunter.

I agree with that feeling to a certain extent. Through the course of a bow season, I will hang 12 to 15 stands on private properties I hunt. I leave these stands until I feel there is a reason to relocate one. However, I have encountered the same good buck out of the same stand on more than one occasion, eventually getting shots at several.

During the season, I usually try to hang an evening stand and hunt it that same day. And I truthfully cannot say that I see more good bucks on the first use of the stand. Personally, I feel that if a hunter takes extra precautions when going to a stand, the wind is right, and the approach to the stand does not pass directly through the travel corridor of the deer, it is possible to hunt the same stand site several times a week without hurting chances for success. Many times I will hang a morning stand the day before the hunt, then be in it come daylight the next day.

When putting out numerous stands for possible future use, I will always do it on a day when it's raining lightly versus a dry, crisp day. I believe that human scent is cleansed from the area more quickly by rain. Likewise, a slow drizzle is one of my favorite hunting times, and unless deer pass directly downwind of the stand, it's doubtful they'll ever know I'm in the area.

When to hunt a stand site is dependent on several factors. First, read the sign and know what's happening in the area. The time to hunt hot rut sign is during the rut . . . not a month later. Second, do your best to determine if the deer in the area of the stand are on a morning or evening pattern. It's amazing what being in that stand at the right time can do to up your chances for success. And third, never hunt an area if the wind is all wrong, no matter how hot the sign or activity. 🦌

STICK IT OUT

by Toby Bridges

Toby's big Minnesota buck

More than a foot of freshly fallen snow made it easy to see where the deer were crossing the long narrow cornfield that snaked along the top of the southeastern Minnesota ridge top. Along the nearly 1-mile length of the field it averaged about 250 yards wide. However, at one point where a deep hollow cut into one side of the ridge, the field narrowed to just a little over a hundred yards across. And it was here that I found the highest concentration of tracks, including several sets of huge imprints that told me they belonged to a big buck or two.

One side of the field rose 50 to 75 feet higher than the opposite side, where it curved around the head of the hollow. A tall straight oak on the high side offered the perfect location for my chain-on stand. Besides offering a lofty vantage point from which I could cover the entire bowl created by the sloping curve of the field, the tree's location insured that I would be downwind from where I anticipated most whitetails to show. With the stand in place, I sat in it the rest of that afternoon with bow in hand – the next morning would be the opener of the general gun season. More than 30 whitetails crossed or fed into the field during the last hour of daylight, including a couple of "shooter" bucks that managed to stay just out of bow range.

It was colder than usual for early November. As our deer camp came alive hours before daybreak the next morning, the local radio station reported that it was a bone-chilling –19 degrees outside, with a windchill of –38 degrees. With more than a mile walk through calf-deep snow ahead of me, I left camp a full hour before the first hint of light. To keep from breaking into a sweat, I wore only a set of fleece pants and jacket over polypropylene underwear. I filled a backpack with additional layers of wool and thermal-insulated clothing, along with a pair of heavily insulated slip-over booties. It took most of that hour to reach my stand, and once I slipped on a few extra layers, staying in that stand the entire day was not all that uncomfortable. By sundown more than a hundred deer had passed within range of my scoped .50-caliber in-line muzzleloader, but the only good buck I saw all day crossed 300 yards down the ridge.

Come daybreak the next morning, I was back in that stand. The warmest it got all day was 11 degrees, with a –20 degree windchill. And still I did not take a shot, although I was tempted to drop a good 140-class 8-pointer that stepped into the field just 50 yards away. But I knew better bucks were in the area, and fortunately held off.

About 9 a.m. the following morning, that same 8-pointer was tempting me again when a beautiful wide-racked 10-pointer suddenly appeared at the edge of the field, then bounded through the deep snow to join a small band of does on the other side. When the deer stopped, it offered a perfect 150-yard broadside shot and my saboted 250-grain bullet found its mark. The 160-class buck traveled only 20 yards before going down, and my long, cold wait was over.

When you have faith in a stand location, stick with it. Always remember that it doesn't matter how many good bucks saunter past it if you're not there to follow through on the reason you hung the stand there in the first place.

TECHNIQUES FOR RECORD-BOOK BUCKS

Choosing the Correct Scrape to Hunt

with Dr. Dave Samuel

Why do whitetail bucks make scrapes? Ask the whitetail-hunting experts featured in this book that question and you'll surely hear two basic answers. Most feel that the primary reason scrapes are made is to allow mature bucks to claim dominance over a particular home range. Scrapes also serve as a means of communication between breeding bucks and receptive estrus does during the rut.

The presence of numerous scrapes within your hunting area can tell you something as well. First, it lets you know that there is a dominant buck in the area, and you've located one of the keys to hunting that deer. Just as importantly, when you find scraping activity in the area you hunt, it is a good indication that the buck-to-doe ratio is within reasonable balance, maybe 1:2 to 1:4. Where does number 6 to 8 for each mature male, bucks commonly do not make many scrapes. Since there are so many does, they don't have to advertise.

How many times have you heard a veteran deer hunter claim that big bucks don't make big scrapes? That when you find a scrape that's as big as the hood of your pickup it was made by numerous young bucks and not the dominant, mature buck of the area? That older bucks seldom visit a scrape once it's made, choosing to only wind-check the scrape from 50 to 75 yards downwind instead? That only bucks make scrapes? Well, there are as many myths about scrapes as there are known truths.

Researchers at the University of Georgia studied ten groups of whitetails for a period of 4 years and discovered that the vast majority of scrapes were made by bucks 3½ years of age and older. Each year, these groups were mixed to make up new groups, but the findings were the same year after year – older bucks conduct nearly all scrape activity.

Noted whitetail authority Dr. Dave Samuel states, "It is probably true that younger bucks make smaller

Dave Samuel with a fine Iowa buck

scrapes. But mature bucks will come back to their *primary* or active scrapes again and again, pawing them and scenting each time, enlarging the scrape with each visit. Keying in on these mature buck scrapes (which are made by 3½- to 5½-year-old deer) will help in harvesting a trophy deer. I have found that these older bucks will use traditional scrapes year after year."

Depending on who you ask, there are three or four different types of scrapes. Some recognize boundary scrapes, which may be found along the boundary of terrain edges or even along the edge of a buck's territory. Then there is what is commonly referred to as the travel-lane scrape, which may mark a travel route from a bedding to a feeding area, or to breeding areas. Trail scrapes are generally a series of small scrapes marking a buck's trail that runs parallel with a more distinct trail favored by the does and young of the year. The so-called breeding scrape is recognized as the "primary scrape," and is the scrape most whitetail hunters focus on.

Contrary to popular belief, not all active scrapes involve an overhanging licking branch. More than once, I have encountered very active scrapes isolated from any foliage whatsoever. I especially remember a scrape in northern Missouri one fall that was as large as my living room. The scraped-up circle was located far out in a huge area of native grasses, nearly a half-mile from the nearest tree. Several times I watched through binoculars as different good, mature bucks worked this open-country scrape.

Most breeding or primary scrapes, however, will feature an overhanging branch which the deer readily mouth, lick and rub with their foreheads, depositing additional scent to communicate with other deer. Whitetails will often establish licking branches throughout much of the year, indicating that they indeed serve as means of keeping in contact with other deer sharing the area. If you find a licking branch that's been visibly chewed on, it's a good bet that during the strong pre-rut you'll find a primary scrape nearby, usually right under the branch.

As a rule, breeding scrapes are most active just before and during the first few days of the rut. Does in estrus will locate and urinate in active scrapes to let the dominant buck know that she is ready or about ready to breed. The dominant buck of the area will also urinate in the scrapes, very often holding his hind legs together so the urine passes through and over the tarsal glands that are located on the inside of each back leg. The strong scent of the rutting buck's urine and tarsal glands tells a receptive doe that he is the boss buck and the one that will do the breeding in this area.

The key to hunting a primary or breeding scrape is to locate one that is being frequented by both a dominant buck and the does of the area. One place to begin your search for a dominant scrape is in fairly open woods with little if any underbrush, allowing deer to visually check the area. Close by you'll usually find heavy cover, allowing a season-wise old buck to slip secretively into the scrape location. Valley bottoms or open flats that extend along one or both sides of a sizeable creek or small river near the end of a brushy point are as good as it gets when you're looking for a very active breeding scrape.

When selecting a bowhunting stand, rarely will I position my stand right over the scrape. Many times, I can't even see the scrape location from the stand site. Smart old bucks will very often approach a scrape from downwind. If they can check the scrape by sniffing the wind currents, they may stay back 50 or 75 yards. If there has not been any activity, they probably will move on to another scrape.

If you know the predominate wind for your hunting area, and you should, look for a good stand location downwind from the scrape. A buck usually approaches a scrape from downwind, so look for his tracks. And since the bucks during this period are often traveling along a line of scrapes, this is where you'll find the big rubs that only trophy-class whitetails can make.

Truly mature bucks of 4 1/2 years of age and older may only physically visit a scrape to freshen it under the cover of darkness. However, these same deer may begin to move more in the last light of evening and first light of morning as the urgency of the oncoming rut causes them to take chances when searching for a hot doe. Still, they are reluctant to walk right up to a scrape during daylight hours. The hunter looking to take one of these deer will enjoy better success hunting on the downwind side of a breeding scrape, and will have to stick with the stand until the last light of day.

If you've located three or four large primary scrapes that establish a pattern that resembles something of a line, you may enjoy greater success on big bucks by focusing more on bottlenecks or funnels along the travel route leading to each of these scrapes. Look for areas where the terrain or land features work to concentrate a buck's movement. If a buck is working a line of scrapes along a wide valley bottom, look for areas where a point extends far into the valley. Along the top of a steep ridge, deer will commonly go around the head of a steep-sided hollow rather than traverse up and down the sharp sides. And where a long narrow cove from a lake or other body of water juts back into the deer cover, whitetails will move around the end of it rather than swim. These are all great places to hang a treestand or build a ground blind.

Scrape activity tails off quickly as the rut progresses and peaks. This is especially true where does greatly outnumber bucks. Once a buck gets with a doe that's nearing estrus, he may stick with her for several days. Then once he has bred the doe, he immediately begins cruising from doe group to doe group to pick up the scent of another receptive mate. Little attention is paid to scrapes.

As the rut begins to die down and it become harder and harder for the buck to find a doe in heat, he will often open up scrapes again for a short period. Fortunately for the deer hunter, not all does are bred during the primary rut. In 25 to 27 days following the start of the rut, those does that were not bred will enter estrus once more. This secondary rut is a less dramatic event, but it does invoke another round of scrape activity, giving the serious whitetail hunter one more chance at the big buck that may have eluded him during the earlier primary rut.

MAKING MOCK SCRAPES

by Gary Clancy

Gary Clancy with a Montana early-season velvet-clad trophy

Why bother making mock scrapes when there are usually plenty of real scrapes to hunt over? That's a legitimate question, and the answer depends on time. Most of us are pressed for time. We consider every minute we're able to be in the woods during the season to be precious. Compared to hunting over mock scrapes, hunting over real scrapes takes too much time.

First, you have to wait for the bucks to begin pawing out their own scrapes. That takes time. Second, you have to scout to find those scrapes. That also takes time – and in addition means you have to prowl around your hunting area to find those scrapes. Big bucks don't do well with prowlers. Then you have to check and recheck those scrapes to make sure the bucks

are continuing to work them. This means more time invested. Finally, you hang your stand and actually get to hunt, hoping all the while that the buck or bucks using the scrape don't suddenly abandon it – which, by the way, happens often. When it comes to time expenditure, hunting natural scrapes is not nearly as "cost effective" as hunting mock scrapes.

In my home hunting area, I like to begin making mock scrapes in September. I make them along trails, old logging roads and the spines of ridges, as well as in creek bottoms and anywhere that sign indicates good deer movement. When I'm in familiar country, I make them along travel routes where I know bucks have scraped in previous years.

Rarely do I make a single mock scrape. Sure,

a buck or two might visit a lone scrape, but putting out a string of scrapes and letting the bucks play "connect-the-dots" is far more effective. How many mock scrapes I employ depends upon the length of the trail or terrain feature I'm hunting. I've used as few as 3 and as many as 20; it just depends upon the situation. I've learned that if you leave too much space between scrapes, bucks are prone to lose interest and wander off. Anything more than 75 yards between scrapes is stretching it. If in doubt, always go closer; it's a little more work, but it's worth it.

How to Build Mock Scrapes

Finding a overhanging branch is the most important part of making any mock scrape. Naturally, when you are making a mock scrape every 50 yards or so, you aren't going to find

overhanging branches right where you need them every time. If you can't find an existing branch, cut a live branch about as big around as your thumb at the base end. I've used branches from maple, oak, ash, basswood, apple, plum, cherry, hickory, cedar, Russian olive and willow, and I haven't noticed any preference by the deer.

(A) Find a good overhanging branch or attach a cut branch to an existing branch with a 12-inch dark plastic tie. These ties are available at any hardware store. The bottom of the branch should be about 5 feet off the ground. Bucks will work lower branches, and I've even seen them stand up on their hind legs to reach higher branches, but the idea here is to make the branch as appealing as possible. Be sure to spray the tips of the branch with a forehead-gland scent.

(B) Beneath the overhanging branch, clear all the forest debris and grass from a spot about the size of a laundry basket. I use a garden trowel to

(A) Spray the overhanging branch with forehead scent. The branch should be 4 to 5 feet above the ground.

(B) Trawl the ground below the branch and add a long-lasting scent to the soil.

work up the soil. Pour a cup or so of Hunter Specialties "Primetime Magic Scrape" (or another commercially available scrape-scent mix) into the dirt. Bucks find this scent-impregnated soil very appealing. In the center make a depression and add about a half-ounce of your favorite liquid scent. You can use urine from doe or buck. I've found both to be equally effective.

(C) At the mock scrape nearest my stand, I take special care because I want a buck to linger here as long as possible to offer me the best opportunity for a shot. I use a scent wick on the overhanging branch and doctor it with fresh forehead-gland scent each time I visit the scrape. Bucks sometimes spend a lot of time sniffing and licking these scent wicks.

(D) Make the scrape itself more appealing by burying scent an inch or two under the soil. You can do this in a couple of different ways. One is to take a glass jar (baby-food jars work well) of

scent, poke some holes in the top and bury the jar. You can also use a 35mm film canister stuffed with clean cotton to which you've added your favorite liquid scent. Another option is to bury one or two scent wafers. The buried scent will ooze appealing odor for weeks.

When doing this work anywhere you are hoping to attract deer, always wear scent-free rubber boots and rubber gloves. Avoid bare-skin contact with anything near the location of the mock scrape.

There's no need to check or freshen your entire string of mock scrapes. The bucks will do that for you. If bucks have not found and begun to work your mock-scrape line within a week or 10 days, look for a better location and establish another line.

(C) Attach a scent wick and spray fresh forehead scent each time you hunt the area.

(D) Bury a soaked scent wafer or other scent holder in the scrape nearest your stand.

Hunting Whitetails on Foot

with Jim Shockey

Canadian big-buck hunter Jim Shockey will be the last person to argue against the effectiveness of patiently hunting whitetails from a carefully positioned treestand. More big bucks are annually taken by this tactic than all others put together. However, this successful trophy-buck hunter also knows there are many times when a hunter will have to take the action to the deer, to get on the ground and seek them out. It's then time to practice the art known as stillhunting.

Hunting whitetails on foot is more than strolling through the woods hoping to see deer. To successfully hunt deer while on the move requires that the hunter develop a discipline which conditions him or her to be continually on the alert – to see the deer before the deer ever knows the hunter is nearby, or get a shot at a good buck that may have already detected that a human has invaded its domain and is in the process of departing the area. When pursuing whitetails at their level, you must always keep your purpose in mind, and remain 100 percent focused, or all you're apt to see will be white tails flagging the exodus of deer that pegged your presence before you ever knew they were there.

"To stillhunt effectively, a hunter must move without appearing to move, and the only way to do this is to move slowly – very slowly. Even when the trees are swaying, or it's raining, masking to some extent the hunter's movement, slowness is the key. And that applies to every movement. Many hunters move their legs slowly, but flip their heads this way and that looking for deer. Not only will a deer pick up on the motion, but it won't be sticking around to find out what was making that motion," declares Shockey.

While Shockey is a firm believer in using a good pair of binoculars to study forms back in the brush, or to check out small pockets of cover he can see without having to enter them, he also feels that hunters use far too much hand movement when continuously grabbing the glasses and bringing them up to their eyes. He points out that it is a natural tendency for hunters to grab binoculars and ram them to their eyes when spotting nearly every flicker of movement. Jim feels that the stand hunter may be able to get away with such motions, but many times the stillhunter who is trying to sneak up on deer won't.

"If you slipped up on the deer properly, you did so by moving slowly and the deer shouldn't know you are there. So what is the hurry? Bring your glasses up to your eyes as slowly as you can. It hurts, believe me. It goes against everything your instincts tell you to do. But you do have the time. So take it. If you do have to hurry to lift your binoculars up, then you must have scared the deer already. And if that is the case, no matter how quick you are, it's too late!" advises Shockey.

While on the topic of binoculars, Jim Shockey claims that the stillhunter who heads out without them pretty well kisses away 50 percent of his chances at being successful. Binoculars enable a hunter to see much farther back into the trees and underbrush than is possible with the naked eye. Tiny gaps in the trees, only an inch or two across, suddenly leap out like so many shooting lanes when a hunter views them through crisp, clear binoculars.

"When it comes to the right pace for stillhunting, it is difficult to put into miles per hour. Every situation calls for a different action, but to give you an idea, if I believe an animal is close by – within several yards – I might take two slow steps every minute or so and stand still the rest of the time. In a day, that speed translates to a traveled distance of several hundred yards, no more. If I do it right and the wind favors me, several hundred yards are enough. It will mean I have penetrated directly to where I believe the buck to be. If he was there, I should have had a crack at him – and if he wasn't there, no big deal. Sure, I could cover a lot more territory by walking faster and not wasting a whole day on one patch of timber. But if a buck had been in those woods, likely all I would have seen of him would have been a brief glimpse of his tail," shares Shockey.

Jim has taken dozens of record-book bucks while stillhunting and says that the only way a hunter can mentally make himself avoid stepping on a dead twig or making the wrong movement is to continually believe that deer are close by. The hunter who doesn't maintain this level of care and awareness will find stillhunting a very tedious, frustrating and unsuccessful way to hunt for whitetails.

For those with the wrong frame of mind for still-hunting or stalking, Shockey says, "Sitting in your comfortable treestand for 2 weeks will seem like a holiday compared with stillhunting 400 acres in a whole day, through woods that may or may not hold a buck."

This hunter has accepted the fact that stillhunting is like making a day-long stalk on an animal that he not only hasn't seen, but also might not even be there. He feels that it is a great test of the hunter's self-discipline. And he will freely admit that he has blown more opportunities than he cares to remember. He says too often he has stopped believing there was a buck ahead. And this generally leads to moving faster through areas he determines to be deerless.

"Sometimes I'm right, and I tell myself 'I told you so,' and head for the next patch of timber to try and salvage what is left of the day. But when I'm wrong, I know immediately that I may have just blown the best opportunity I might get. The deer are where they are – not where you think they should be!" Shockey shares.

Jim feels that the entire idea of stillhunting is not radically different than hunting from a stand located on the ground. He says the difference in these hunting styles is that the stillhunter actively penetrates where the deer may be bedded. The biggest drawback is that the stillhunter must move to get within range, and when he does move he risks

detection. He attributes the high success of stand hunting, whether it's from the ground or from a treestand, to the fact that the hunter doesn't have to move.

Wind can cause whitetails to hole up and prevent them from moving. For Shockey, windy conditions mean he's more likely to find the deer where he expects them to be, in their beds. Windy weather conditions are some of his favorite times to be slipping slowly and quietly through deer cover.

"A windy day is not the only way to get out and sneak through the forest – it just happens to be the easiest way to recognize a day to stillhunt," he says.

Wind and rain are two major weather factors which can present the perfect window for making a stillhunt into cover that could hold a trophy buck. One thing is for certain – when it's extremely windy or when periods of rain drench the woods, the whitetails' senses of smell, hearing and even sight become somewhat neutralized. Strong gusts of wind scatter scent molecules in every direction, and a buck that picks up human odor may not have the slightest idea of the direction from which it came. Likewise, a slow, steady rain can keep scent cleansed from the air, and close to the hunter. And when the wind has the treetops and lower branches constantly moving, the motion and natural sounds can effectively mask the soft noises and movement of an approaching hunter.

"If the hunter uses common sense, then he can decide which days are best suited for stillhunting and which days he would be better off waiting in a tree for the deer to come to him. By relying on both of these hunting techniques, a hunter greatly increases his efficiency and will increase the number of deer he sees over the duration of the season," proclaims Shockey.

Still, he knows that there are times when the hunter looking to take a really good buck will do better stillhunting even though the conditions are only marginal. The period of the season can largely dictate whether a hunter should be pursuing his buck on foot or waiting in ambush.

Shockey realizes that early in the season, bucks may not move much at all. They're still not out actively pursuing does, and food may be plentiful right where they're bedding. A hunter could spend a great deal of time in a treestand and never see these bucks, even though a buck may be spending all of his time on just a few acres of cover less than a half-mile away. This is a prime

Fresh snow often allows for ideal stillhunting.

example of when the hunter may have to take the hunt to a sedentary buck.

"A hunter also must consider that if he penetrates any distance into a buck's private domain, the buck will know it. Either the hunter will kill the buck or, far more likely, the buck will escape. Just as surely, no matter what happens, the chances of the buck being in the vicinity the next day is slim. Stillhunting can ruin a good set-up for stand hunting, so I keep several locations available for stillhunting only. If I spoil one area, I can leave it for a few days while I hunt my other areas. And I never stillhunt where I standhunt," Shockey warns.

Why should a hunter risk failure when he can sit in a tree and eventually enjoy a high degree of success? Sure, there are those days when getting down onto the ground and seeking out the deer will be the only way you can make things happen. Then there are those days when the timing of the season dictate that stillhunting is likely to be the most successful way to get a buck in your sights. But for Jim, the technique puts more emphasis on hunting than on waiting.

"When you are stillhunting, you are hunting. You are actively searching out your prey, matching your skill and expertise with the far superior ability of the whitetail deer," concludes Shockey.

In the following pages of this chapter we will take a good look at the clothing, footwear and other equipment that can add to the success of a properly conducted stillhunt.

Successful Stillhunting Begins with Proper Wear

The reward of getting a shot at a nice buck during a long morning, afternoon or entire day of slowly easing through the deer woods can hinge on the stillhunter's choice of clothing. It is truly a case of the clothing making the man, or in this case, making the hunter!

Clothing

If your plans for the day include stillhunting, avoid wearing outerwear with a hard or slick surface. Every branch that slides across materials such as nylon or many other outer-shell materials with a high synthetic content can send a warning signal the deer may pick up on long before you're within sighting distance. With some of the worst material choices, just human movement can result in a very audible "swishing" sound.

Wool outerwear was always been a favorite with successful stillhunters of the past, and remains popular with many of today's hunters on the go. However, the naturally quiet material does have a few drawbacks. For one thing, heavy wool clothing in extreme cold can really weigh a hunter down. Also, a thick wool jacket doesn't tend to have the give or flex of most modern materials, making it more difficult for a hunter to move effortlessly through thick cover. However, some of the newer wool/synthetic blends are proving to be softer and more pliable, providing both the warmth for hunting in colder weather and silence when a hunter in stealth mode accidentally rubs up against a tree branch or sapling trunk.

Some of the modern fleece-type materials seem to have been designed primarily with the stillhunter in mind. Made of long-wearing and easy-care polyester or nylon that has been specially spun to produce a super-soft, almost suede-like whisper-quiet surface, fleece is the answer when weight becomes a real concern. Even "heavyweight" fleece wear is commonly as light as a feather. Fleece outerwear can be slipped on over practically nothing during warm-weather hunts, or looser-fitting fleece pants and jacket can be slipped over several layers of

Jim Shockey with a Canadian monster

thermal undergarments for comfort when temperatures begin to plummet.

Another popular material among hunters looking for exceptional quietness in the clothing they wear has been Saddlecloth. This multi-layer material incorporates a fine membrane of Teflon that helps keep the bite of cold wind out, and can even keep a hunter from getting drenched when an unexpected shower dampens the deer woods. The material features a brushed surface that's exceptionally quiet, making clothing made from Saddlecloth extremely popular with both bowhunters and stillhunters.

While a light rain can offer the stillhunter some of the quietest conditions in which to hunt, most of the rainwear available to hunters can be best described as being on the noisy side. Vinyl-surfaced and slick nylon raingear can be far too noisy to wear while sneaking through the woods, and some of the rainwear that features an internal waterproof plastic lining often isn't much better. Choose rainwear for stillhunting very carefully, and be prepared to pay a pretty penny for it. Good raingear is expensive, but should be considered an investment, not an expense.

Where legal, camouflaged outerwear or blaze-orange camouflaged wear will help mask a hunter's movement. If the state you hunt requires at least a solid orange vest during the firearms and/or muzzleloader seasons, choose one made of quiet fleece. It doesn't do much good to be fully decked out in clothing made of quiet cloth, then slip on a noisy, hard-surfaced nylon or plastic fluorescent orange vest.

Footwear

Jim Shockey spends most of his fall and early winter pursuing the big bucks of Saskatchewan and Alberta. In this country, heavy snow can cover the ground by the first of November and temperatures can nosedive to well below zero. Would you believe that this successful stillhunter can often be found stillhunting in socks?

When the snows are deep and the temperatures cold enough to eliminate moisture, Shockey very often slips on several pairs of wool socks and an insulated bootie, then tops everything with a very heavy wool outer sock. Jim does not intend to walk for miles when stillhunting, and in an entire day he may cover no more than a few hundred yards. His choice of footwear allows him to feel things underfoot, such as a dead branch just under the surface of the snow.

When selecting footwear specifically for stillhunting, choose carefully. Avoid boots with a stiff outer sole that can snap branches before you ever know they are underfoot. In warm weather, go with the lightest boot possible. Light boots allow more precise placement of the foot, and thin, flexible soles permit some feel of what's beneath your step before applying enough pressure to snap a branch. In colder weather, you may have to revert to insulated pac boots or heavily insulated rubber boots. While soles with aggressive tread designs may offer greater traction on slick surfaces, these soles also tend to be stiffer and less forgiving when you walk across things that can snap and give away your presence. Soles with rounded edges also tend to be more forgiving than soles with a sharp edge.

Binoculars

Experienced stillhunters feel no more fully dressed without a pair of good binoculars around their neck than they would without the proper outerwear. Medium-sized glasses of 7- to 10-power magnification are best suited for carrying all day, while still providing good light-gathering and clarity.

Those models featuring small 20mm to 25mm front lenses usually make for an exceptionally light pair of binoculars that are barely noticeable around the neck, but due to the small size of the front glass these are generally difficult to see through clearly in low-light conditions. On the other hand, bigger binoculars with 50mm or larger front lenses may offer exceptional light-gathering capabilities, but can weigh so much it's like carrying an anvil around your neck. Concentrate on those binoculars with 30mm to 40mm front lenses. As a rule these offer the best of both worlds – acceptable clarity and definition in poor light, while still being tolerable to carry all day long.

A number of manufacturers offer a harness that keeps the glasses tight to your chest, preventing them from bouncing around and whacking you as you stillhunt through thick cover. These harnesses also put the weight of the binoculars on your shoulders instead of your neck. At a cost of around $20, these harnesses are a fantastic bargain.

"LOOKING-GLASS" WHITETAILS

by Toby Bridges

Nothing had moved past my stand location in three mornings. Other hunters in our northern Missouri hunting camp were experiencing the same thing. The deer simply were not moving, most likely due to a prolonged rainy low-pressure front that just would not go away. My stand was in a great spot, but after sitting in it for 3 hours the third morning of the general firearms season without seeing a single deer, I had become tired of waiting for the deer to come to me. I decided that it was time to hit the ground and try taking the action to the deer.

One advantage of the wet weather was the silent walking. Soaked from nearly a week of rain, the forest floor was as quiet to walk on as carpet, allowing me to slip noiselessly along the hardwood-covered ridges and points. Since no one was seeing deer moving on their own, I didn't expect to spot any more natural movement just because I was on the move. Instead, I concentrated on spotting deer that were bedded. And instead of relying on only my eyes to dissect the terrain, I constantly picked apart every feature of adjacent points, steep slopes and valley bottoms through a quality pair of binoculars.

Four hours after setting out on foot, I had covered just a little more than a half-mile. But in that distance, I had glassed deer five times. However, only one had been a buck, a small 6-pointer that was on the prowl. The others had consisted of mother doe and fawn groups. Twice, I knew the deer had also spotted me, but due to my extremely slow progress, the deer never got up from their beds. However, as long as I was in sight, they never took their eyes off of me.

After breaking for about 15 minutes to enjoy a sandwich and candy bar lunch, I headed down a steep point into a brushy valley below. My plans were to slowly work back towards camp a mile away. If I hunted at the same snail's pace I had used since leaving my stand, I knew I would end up in the last light of day in a field less than a quarter-mile from the old farm house where we stayed.

I progressed along, three, four or five steps at a time. Then I would stand still for 3 or 4 minutes, studying the cover around me for the slightest movement or out-of-place feature. About every third or fourth stop, I'd slowly and methodically glass everything in sight. Looking through my Nikon 8-power binoculars allowed me to concentrate on each small piece of prime white-tail estate, and carefully pick apart what definitely did not look like a deer from what sort of looked like a deer. Twice in the next several hours, I spotted whitetails before they spotted me. Unfortunately, none of these deer were shooters.

The gloom of the heavily overcast sky meant it would become dark early, and I was just beginning to lose good light when suddenly, through the binoculars, I distinguished a couple of deer legs among a stand of saplings. A tiny movement had alerted me to the whitetail's presence, and after a closer examination, I could make out a nice main beam, then a few points. After a minute more of study, I knew I was looking at a good buck.

The deer had no idea I was anywhere in the area, although I was less than 75 yards from where he stood. When he dropped his head, I made a few slow steps toward a sizeable oak tree. I eased my Savage muzzleloader around the trunk, resting the forearm on my hand. Through the variable scope, set at 4-power, I searched for an opening. Miraculously, it was there. I centered the crosshairs directly on the buck's shoulder, and sent a saboted 250-grain bullet through the 10-inch window.

That 150-class 10-pointer now hangs on the wall behind me, looking over my shoulder as I write this. Every time I look up at the deer, I think back to that rainy day when I had to take the action to the deer – spending most of the day in slow motion and peering through a looking glass.

HANDLING THE NOISE FACTOR

by Toby Bridges

When dry conditions persist, and the woods floor is covered with a heavy layer of wind- and sun-dried leaves, trying to sneak along quietly is like trying to slip up on someone across a floor covered with cornflakes. It presents a real challenge for even the best stillhunter.

However, keep in mind that everything that walks in the woods will make noise when it's this dry, whether it's deer, turkeys, squirrels, chipmunks or raccoons. Anything that stirs will make noise. So it simply stands to reason that the best way to handle the noise factor is to try your darnedest to sound more like a woods critter than a human. And the way to do this is to move slowly, taking only a few steps at a time, then stopping for several minutes or longer, as if to ponder the next move or to look for danger – just like another deer.

Most humans stop very little when walking through the woods, and the rhythm of their fast-paced footsteps can usually be easily distinguished from the walking of most wildlife. Even when trying to ease through the woods, the majority of hunters characteristically take twenty to thirty steps before pausing to look around, and the breaks in their cadence are generally very short. Every deer in the woods soon knows when most hunters enter their domain.

Sometimes three or four wild turkeys walking through dry leaves at the same time can sound surprisingly like a couple of hunters. However, as turkeys ease through the fall woods, they very often make very soft purrs and clucks to one another, and the deer also pick up on these sounds, realizing that the footsteps they hear are nothing to fear. Fortunately, the cautious hunter can just as easily make this same soft turkey talk with a mouth-operated diaphragm turkey call.

I can remember one particular Missouri muzzleloader season when the woods were so dry it was virtually impossible to reach any of my stands without alerting every deer in the woods I had arrived. After 3 days of spotting white flags flying through the hardwoods ahead of me or far down the points running from the ridge tops, I decided to try masking the sounds of my footsteps with yelps and clucks from a diaphragm call. But I never did make it to my stand.

The first afternoon I tried the tactic, I was slowly easing down a ridge toward a distant stand site. I had left my pickup extremely early in the afternoon in order to make the long 3/4-mile walk, two and three carefully planned steps at a time. Even as slowly as I inched closer and closer toward the stand, leaves crunched loudly underfoot.

I'd make a couple of steps, then yelp or cluck a few times with the call pushed up into the roof of my mouth. About halfway to the treestand, I watched as a doe and two fawns eased up a point and crossed less than a hundred yards from where I watched around the trunk of a huge oak. The deer were not at all alarmed, even though I had just stopped walking in the dry leaves only seconds before spotting them.

As soon as the deer disappeared on down a point on the opposite side of the ridge, I began moving again – still clucking and lightly yelping with the call. Another hundred yards past where the doe and fawns had crossed, I had just stopped moving my feet when I heard another set of footsteps. I knew immediately it was the sound of a lone deer coming up the steep side of the ridge. Then suddenly a beautiful 8-pointer walked right into sight just 60 yards away, offering an easy shot for my in-line muzzleloading rifle.

Since that first afternoon of success, I have always made sure there is a diaphragm turkey call in a breast pocket before heading into the woods for a morning or afternoon of deer hunting, whether I plan to spend the time in a favorite stand or moving about. Many times in the past, I had heard of hunters pulling a drag rope behind them as they stillhunted. The dragging sound of the rope would supposedly mask the sounds of their footsteps. And the tactic may work just fine, but for me it'll always be the use of a turkey call if wild turkeys are native to the area I'm hunting.

Minnesota bowhunter Jeff Ottosen with a massive October whitetail

TECHNIQUES FOR RECORD-BOOK BUCKS

Beyond the Grunt Call

with Stan Potts

The grunt call of a whitetail buck is easily the most widely recognized sound made by a whitetail deer. However, it is not the only vocal sound made by deer or used in their daily communications or interactions with other deer. Other sounds, or calls, heard regularly include the fawn or doe bleat and the snort. And while the number of different sounds made by whitetails may be very limited, deer-hunting experts are now realizing that it is often the tone or emphasis put on a grunt, bleat or snort that actually determines its meaning or purpose.

Many experienced deer hunters are no longer content to just sit in ambush, waiting for a good buck to materialize. Instead, they are now calling to the deer in order to up their odds of eventually getting a high-horned buck within range. One of those hunters is renowned Illinois bowhunter Stan Potts, who has a number of record-book-class whitetails to his credit, including a tremendous buck that for several decades held the number-two spot in his state for typical archery-taken white-tails. Potts has become a firm believer in talking to the deer.

"I have been whitetail-deer hunting for over 30 years, but it wasn't until about 1990 that I started calling deer seriously. I've found that it can work for you all season long. But while you can expect a lot of success, you cannot expect a deer to come to your calling all the time. That's okay, though,

because that one time a big buck does come in, it will be like no other feeling you've ever had!" states Potts.

Like all serious big-buck hunters, Stan lives for a strong pre-rut period. He feels that this is when good bucks become more vulnerable, and are the most callable. And as you might suspect, at this time of the year he relies more on the various grunt calls than on other vocal sounds. He says that knowing which grunt call to use then becomes the key to success.

Potts recognizes that bucks make grunts with varying sounds, tones or volumes at different times. Not all grunts are the same, nor do they have the same meaning. For this very successful bowhunter, one of the best times to call deer is when bucks are running a scrape line.

Stan explains, "As the buck does so, he will usually grunt softly every 30 . . . 40 . . . 50 yards. When a hunter spots a buck working scrapes, the grunt calls he makes should not be too aggressive. But neither should the hunter be afraid to call. When the calls are kept soft, often the buck will come in, mostly because he's curious. He wants to find out who the other buck is and where he fits into the pecking order."

He goes on to share that when a buck is in hot pursuit of a doe in estrus, the grunts can become very excited, drawn out and repetitive – almost nonstop. These are generally referred to as tending grunts. Then there are also inquisitive grunts, which tend to ask, "Where are you?" And the very aggressive challenge grunt can acknowledge that another buck has trespassed into territory where he's not welcomed.

"Whitetail bucks can become quite vocal before and during the rut. The times to make a particular grunt sound can be learned only through experience in the deer woods, and just how these calls should sound from hearing them either firsthand or from experts who have mastered the calls," claims Potts.

American Indians learned long ago that a hunter could call deer within bow range by imitating the bleats of a fawn or doe. Both calls can be just as deadly today as they were hundreds of years ago. The fawn bleat is generally considered a distress call, especially when the hunter puts a little feeling into the sound. It says, "I need help!" These calls play on the maternal instincts of does, and practically all adult does will respond to the plea. And when a doe responds to the call, especially in the pre-rut or rut, there could be a good buck following right behind her.

"The fawn bleat not only calls in the does, but often a buck will respond as well, perhaps out of curiosity, or maybe to make sure that all is okay," says Potts.

Bleat call

The bleat of an adult doe normally doesn't get quite the attention of the distress bleats of a yearling fawn, but it can have its place and time to attract other deer. Potts says that any "non-alert" call can be a successful part of calling deer. He acknowledges that deer are extremely curious animals and will often come to investigate any deer sound that does not signal danger.

Many experienced deer callers will include what is known as the doe estrus bleat in their repertoire of calls while attempting to call in a rutting buck, mixing in tending grunts. The doe's estrus bleat is often referred to as the doe grunt, and is higher pitched and slightly longer than the common

doe bleat. This can be a great call to use when the rut has started to wind down and bucks are finding it harder to find a hot doe. And like bucks, does also have a pecking order, with the most dominant does often the most vocal. When bleats from a subordinate fill the woods, very often a dominant doe will come to investigate who dared to break this pecking order.

"I use the fawn and doe bleats a lot, especially during the early part of the season before the bucks begin to lust after the does. I like to call in and harvest does, both because I'm into quality deer management and recognize the need for doe harvest – and because this is also the best time to harvest does for the freezer. Later in the season I want to be concentrating on hunting big bucks, and then I like some of those does around to lure bucks to my stand area during the pre-rut and rut," remarks Potts.

He adds, "The doe estrus bleat is one of the deadliest calls you can use during the rut, yet it is one of the most underutilized. It's a sound a doe makes when she is ready to be bred, but there isn't an eligible buck close by. Combine this with the fact that this is the time of the year when bucks are aggressively trolling for hot does, and it makes sense that when they hear this sound they often come to it on a run. It has worked for me many times."

The snort is a call that's mostly associated with danger. The sound is made by practically all deer, both bucks and does, and is the result of a deer blowing hard through its nostrils to free them of foreign matter or mucus, or perhaps the strong smell of whatever it may have been feeding on. This sudden reverse of air causes the fine hairs inside the nasal passage to stand upright, making the sense of smell more acute. It allows the deer's olfactory system to precisely pinpoint sources of odor. While a few experienced deer hunters claim there are variations of the snort that may signify different degrees of alarm, the sound is nonetheless always associated with

Stan Potts learned the subtle calls that deer make by spending time in the woods.

danger. Most hunters simply eliminate the sound from their list of calls. However, a few, more daring callers now combine something of a snort-wheeze which can serve as a challenge to another buck.

"Like all hunting techniques, deer calling does not work each and every time. Calling is not a magical, no-fail bag of tricks that can overcome sloppy hunting techniques, poor stand site selection or failure to control human scent. However, the whitetail hunter who is headed into the woods without a grunt tube and doe bleat call is not giving himself the maximum opportunity to be successful. Deer calling is super exciting, and at the right time can be pure poison on the largest bucks," advises Potts.

Choose a Good Calling Location

"Always remember that a deer that comes to your call is looking for the other deer that is calling to him," says Potts.

With that in mind, this very successful deer-calling expert pays special attention to his location before attempting to call. He knows the importance of creating a set-up that forces the buck to expose himself as the deer looks for the source of the calling. He is also quick to point out that a wary older buck will often avoid sauntering into the open, readily exposing himself. When calling to mature bucks, the hunter must always be on the alert, searching with his or her eyes to detect the smallest flicker of movement back in the heavy cover.

"Always make sure you have a shot window on the downwind side of your stand. Whitetails, especially good bucks, will most always try to circle downwind of the calling in an attempt to locate the other deer with their keen sense of smell," advises Potts.

One way to keep a buck from circling your calling location is to set up where the deer either can't come in from that side or where doing so means that a buck may have to leave the comfort zone of thick, protective cover. In the latter situation, secretive trophy-class bucks may tend to remain in the heavy cover that's ideally upwind and directly in front of your calling and shooting position.

"Here is a good example of a great calling location," says Stan Potts, adding, "Say you place your stand up against a steep bluff, or at the edge of a steep drop-off, where a buck cannot easily get around behind you as he responds to your calling. Be sure to pay special attention to swirling wind currents when hunting severe structure like this. Any buck that comes to the calling will most likely work out away from the vertical wall or sharp drop-off. And if there is a line of heavy cover a short ways in front of your stand, there is a very good chance that the deer will either work right along its edge or just inside the line of cover. A couple of carefully cut shooting lanes can put a buck right where you want him – in front of your stand and well inside your comfortable shooting range!"

When calling in an area with a high deer density, always keep in mind that it is most often the younger bucks that will respond to your calls first. Many times there may be a bigger buck close by, listening to your calls and carefully plotting his approach in order to check out the luring sounds. However, if one or more of those younger bucks ends up downwind of your location and picks up your scent in the air currents, there's a good chance the morning or afternoon hunt is over.

Experts like Stan generally agree that it is not a good idea to call to spooked whitetails that have picked up your human odor. Most feel that all it does is tend to educate the deer, especially older bucks that seem to already be treading on pins and needles. However, a few hunters have successfully gotten bucks back by waiting 10 to 20 minutes after the deer have left the area, then rattling aggressively, throwing in a few grunts.

The modern centerfire rifle shooter and to a slightly lesser degree the hunter who relies on a scoped modern in-line percussion muzzleloader can easily take deer out at 100 to 200 yards, and possibly farther. While calling location is still important when hunting with these weapons, it's not quite as crucial as when hunting with a bow and arrow, where the deer must usually be within 30 yards. In fact, when care is taken to set up in an ideal calling location, the centerfire rifle hunter who can shoot out to 300 yards may find that he has a 600-yard-wide zone of fire that can practically encircle his location. With good concealment, about the only direction he may not get a shot would be in a 15-to 20-degree angle extending directly downwind of his location.

BEST TIME FOR CALLING

by Mark Drury

I'm a firm believer in calling to whitetails throughout the entire season, from early October on through the last of the season as late as the end of January. Depending on the time of the season, the weather conditions, the amount of hunting pressure that has been put on the deer, and a number of other factors, different types of calls will be more effective than others. However, like other serious hunters who spend most of 3 or 4 months each fall and winter pursuing whitetails, I too have my favorite time of the year to be in a stand. That time is the 10 days to 2 weeks preceding the actual beginning of the breeding period, or rut. I've found that this is when deer are always most susceptible to the use of deer calls.

And even during this time, when bucks tend to be extremely active, I have found periods when I will definitely spend extra hours in the stand. Easily my favorite time occurs when a strong high-pressure front suddenly pushes into one of the Midwestern hot spots I frequent during the pre-rut or the beginning of the rut in early November. The drop in temperature that accompanies this strong frontal movement kicks buck activity into high gear.

During the peak activity periods of late afternoon and early evening, I'll combine a series of grunts with some aggressive rattling, adding now and then a few doe estrus bleats. I've found this technique to be especially effective when I know two or more bucks are in the area, competing for territory and receptive does.

When I've done my homework and have my stand in the right spot, I very often find myself right in the middle of some very hot rutting action. Even when I watch as two mature bucks chase a hot doe, I'll continue calling to them. More than once my efforts have excited the bucks into staging a fight, and sooner or later one of them has to come over to investigate the buck they kept hearing but haven't yet seen.

I call the technique "Power Calling," and my goal is to force some action where I can take advantage of what the deer are already doing naturally. Whether I can see the deer or not, I believe in aggressive calling during the pre-rut and rut periods. I've taken too many good bucks with the technique at this time of the year to have any doubts about just how effectively it works on mature whitetails.

Weather . . . or Not

with Peter Fiduccia

The dedicated big-buck hunter can control many things that directly affect the success of his or her efforts to harvest a trophy-class whitetail deer, including personal scent control, accurate interpretation of the sign found, good stand placement, use of the right hunting equipment and even the discretion to remain quiet about the location of a book-class buck that's been located. However, there remains one very important factor that not even the most experienced whitetail hunter has any control over, and that's the weather.

Depending on where you live and hunt, your idea of perfect deer-hunting weather may vary somewhat. In the Midwest, seasoned deer hunters tend to favor clear, crisp mornings in the upper 20s or lower 30s, with a heavy frost on the ground at daybreak and temperatures warming into the mid-40s by noon. Out West on the high plains, consistently successful whitetail hunters pray for a light snow, while in the South they tend to take what they get and keep their fingers crossed that it isn't a late-season hurricane. But what about deer hunting when, in your mind, the weather is less than ideal?

"Contrary to what most of us are told and believe, hunting deer in bad weather can be productive. Yes, there are times to stay in bed when the weather turns sour, but, generally, deer hunting in the rain or snow can put a buck on the wall and meat in your freezer!" states whitetail hunting expert Peter Fiduccia.

He adds, "After evaluating my foul-weather deer-hunting statistics that I keep regularly each year on my Deer Diary Stat Cards, I have determined that deer, especially bucks, will move during nasty weather."

Peter identifies foul weather, as far as the deer are concerned, as rain, wind, ice, snow, fog, extreme cold, mist and even unusually hot and arid conditions. He points out that each of these conditions trigger a different type of activity response from whitetails. The hunter that learns how to capitalize on hunting during each of these weather conditions can be amazingly successful.

"Except for the most severe and extreme weather conditions, such as a 24-hour blizzard, a severe ice storm or a 12-hour torrential downpour, deer generally won't bed for lengthy periods of time," shares this season-wise whitetail hunter.

The whitetail is a ruminant, which means it has a four-chambered stomach. Each of these stomach compartments is shaped differently, has a different type of lining and serves a different purpose in the digestion of the wide variety of browse, forage and grasses consumed by whitetails. From the moment of ingestion and storage of roughly chewed food in the first of these compartments, it takes approximately 24 to 36 hours for that food to be passed out as dung in an adult deer. That being the case, whitetails cannot totally hole up for much longer than that. They have to move and feed.

"Deer instinctively know they must feed and must do so in spite of a steady rain, windy day or snowy afternoon," states Fiduccia.

"These types of weather conditions give something of an edge to the hunter. I have used a day with gusty winds to sneak up undetected on a buck bedded in laurels or on ledges, or nervously feeding in a woodlot or field," claims Fiduccia.

Peter Fiduccia

This very successful big-buck hunter has developed something of a formula for being successful season after season: CONCENTRATION + POSITIVE THINKING + CONFIDENCE = CONSISTENT SUCCESS. Fiduccia believes that if one element is eliminated from this equation, a hunter seriously reduces his chances of being successful. This is especially true during wet, snowy, windy and bitter cold hunting conditions, for which he employs a second formula: DETERMINATION + PATIENCE + STAMINA + COMFORT = SUCCESS.

"Without these fundamental components, foul-weather hunting is an exercise in futility. That bears repeating. If you leave out any of these factors, the potential for your success drops accordingly. Leave out more than one of any of these factors and the possibility of success is almost nonexistent!" exclaims Fiduccia.

Peter Fiduccia's Foul-Weather Hunting Strategies

"An unusual behavioral trait brought on by bad weather is deer activity at odd times of the day. Generally nocturnal, especially in heavily hunted areas, the whitetail may spend a large part of the day moving just before or after a storm. This activity often intensifies as the storm begins or ends. Dramatic drops or increases in temperature or barometric pressure will also increase deer activity before, during and after a storm. This is especially true if extreme bad-weather conditions have held the deer stationary for a long time," says Fiduccia.

He feels that standhunting and stillhunting remain the best tactics for foul-weather deer hunting, but he says not to expect a little movement here or there. During these conditions Peter says that it becomes a matter of feast or famine – you're likely to see either a lot of deer, or no deer at all. If they are moving, they tend to move continually. However, if they are not traveling, he says it will take additional effort, such as stillhunting or stalking, to slip close to bedded deer or deer that remain in a small, specific area.

When the wind is howling, say around 40 mph, and a storm has been in your hunting area for several hours, chances are the deer will remain bedded until the winds begin to subside, or hunger forces them to begin foraging. Fiduccia feels these periods of strong wind are the ideal times for stillhunting. He says to concentrate on areas of heavy cover. He points out that bucks won't be bedded where they normally bed. Instead, he has learned that they will seek out the thickest

During periods of high winds, a whitetail's senses are not as acute as during calm weather. Everything around it is moving in the wind – leaves and cornstalks are swirling, rustling or constantly swaying back and forth, while tree limbs are in motion and rattling against each other. It becomes extremely difficult for the deer to pick up on a slight movement or hear anything that could be a predator, or a hunter. Gusting winds can also quickly disperse scent molecules, greatly reducing the effectiveness of a whitetail's sensitive nose. A deer's sense of smell, sight and hearing are further reduced when windy conditions are accompanied by rain or snow.

"To be a successful foul-weather deer hunter, one must motivate himself to go hunting on a snowy or rainy day – even during a rainstorm. Without this determination, the battle is lost before it has begun. Once you've convinced yourself to hunt in this type of weather you must be prepared to be in the woods as long as you would if you were hunting on a clear day. Hunting in foul weather demands this type of determination. It will regularly pay off in big dividends," says Fiduccia.

and most impenetrable cover they can find, such as a heavy stand of cedars. During heavy winds and rain, mature bucks often head for standing corn and other "timber-free" hiding places. Fiduccia has found that stillhunting through standing corn during windy conditions can be a productive tactic.

He has observed, "It takes gale-force conditions to put deer down and keep them there. This is primarily attributed to the fact that two of their most relied-on senses – hearing and smell – are significantly reduced during these conditions. Deer try to make up for this deficiency by relying on their other prime sense – sight. To do so, they must stay on the move and always scan their surroundings for activity and danger. Even this becomes difficult when everything in the deer's environment is moving from the blowing wind. Contrary to popular belief, even when high winds are blowing up to 40 mph, deer will continue to move and feed. Taking a stand on the fringe of heavy cover often proves to be a very effective method."

Rain or shine, Peter Fiduccia will be in the deer woods during the hunting season. In some states, the firearms seasons can be relatively short. If you let a few days of bad weather keep you out of the woods during one of these short gun seasons, you could lose a major portion of your hunting opportunity. This is especially true if one of those days happens to be opening day. In many states as much as 60 to 80 percent of all deer harvested during that season are taken on opening day. Miss that day due to rain, snow, sleet or wind and you have cut your chances of being successful by nearly the same percentage. 🦌

DEALING WITH DEEP SNOW

by Dave Maas

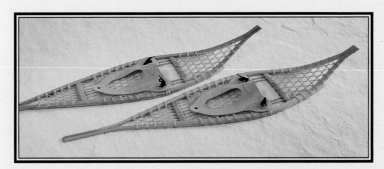

You've heard the saying: "I've got good news and bad news." For where I hunt in eastern South Dakota, the good news is that a heavy snowfall drives whitetails out of the local cattail sloughs and CRP fields of the prairie, and into a half-mile-long wooded creek bottom owned by my in-laws. The bad news is that it's almost impossible to access this property once the snow flies. The nearest plowed road is nearly a mile away, and messing with a trailer and snowmobile is a big (and smelly) hassle, especially in the dark before a morning hunt. It didn't take a rocket scientist to come up with the idea of using snowshoes, but it did take me a few seasons to find the perfect type of snowshoe for hunting. Consider these factors before you buy a pair:

• **Stealth:** Forget about the trendy metal-framed snowshoes – they're noisy and don't provide the flotation of a traditional wood snowshoe when breaking trail on fluffy snow.

• **Shape:** Without a doubt, the Ojibwa-style snowshoe (above) is number one in my book. The pointed tail works as a reliable rudder as you walk, and the pointed toe acts like a ski moving easily through the snow and brush. The pair I own are made in Minnesota by a company called Country Ways (www.snowshoe.com).

• **Length:** Figure out how much weight your snowshoes will be carrying. If the total is from 130 to 250 pounds, buy the 54-inch Ojibwa. If it's over 250, then buy the 60-inchers. Women and other small-sized hunters are best served by the 48-inch model.

• **Bindings:** I prefer flex-rubber bindings for hunting. This design is ideal for quickly slipping the snowshoes on and off without having to remove your gloves to fumble with the tiny (and cold!) metal buckles found on traditional strap-type bindings. You'll especially appreciate these bindings at the end of a frigid morning or evening hunt, when you're chilled to the bone and you can't even feel your fingers.

WHEN YOU'RE HOT, YOU'RE HOT

by Toby Bridges

Probably the toughest hunting conditions a deer hunter can be faced with while trying to hang his tag on a trophy-class whitetail buck arise when unusually hot temperatures coincide with a full moon. In recent years across most of the country, early November has seen temperatures that are often 20 to 30 degrees warmer than normal. And when morning temperatures heat up quickly into the 70s, deer aren't going to be moving much during daylight hours.

Instead, the deer become extremely nocturnal, moving almost entirely at night. This is especially true when there's a full moon lighting up the woods and fields all night long. Sometimes, not even the urgency of the rut can make the deer move until well after the sun has slipped below the western horizon. And when the heat is on, most whitetails will be headed back to their bedding areas before first light.

I can remember one season when such conditions threatened to ruin a long-anticipated high-plains hunt for whitetails. Normally, during the mid-November general rifle season in this particular area, up to a foot of snow covers the ground and temperatures at daybreak hover around 10 degrees, warming to around 25 degrees by midday. This particular year, we left camp in the pre-dawn darkness with little more than a light jacket on, which quickly came off as soon as the sun popped over the distant horizon and pushed temperatures into the mid-70s.

To compound the problem, that year the rut (and the season dates) encompassed the full moon. The only saving grace was that for nearly 2 months prior to the season opener, the area had received less than an inch of rain. Small feeder creeks and waterholes were mostly dry, forcing the deer to make a daily move down to the wide, shallow river that cut through the ranch to quench their thirsts.

Many of the deer simply stayed near the river, holing up in the small woodlots that dotted the numerous hay fields. However, many of the good bucks continued to use familiar bedding areas high up in the oak-covered canyons a mile or two from the only reliable water source, forcing them to make the long trek every evening and back again every morning. Since most of the does had moved down to the river, many of these bucks tended to linger there until first light, hoping to pick up on a hot doe.

Instead of heading to the river bottom where hundreds of deer fed, watered and frolicked all night, each morning found me sitting on a high ridge more than a mile back from all the action. From there, I would glass the narrow valleys and grass-covered ridges leading up to the secluded pockets where many of the bucks would spend the day. It was a tactic that paid off when on the fourth morning I located a good near-150-class 10-pointer as it slowly made its way up one of the points leading to a high ridge.

Some fast footwork allowed me to stay above that buck and get around to where that point topped out. A well-placed shot from my muzzleloader ended the hunt. I had taken a very negative weather-related hunting situation and turned it into a successful hunt. While you can't do anything about the weather, often you can do something about when, where and how you cope with the situation at hand. Sometimes, you have to get creative.

Toby Bridges with a warm-weather buck

MOONLIGHT MADNESS

by Toby Bridges

Easily one of the most misunderstood influences on the whitetail rut is the effect that different moon phases have on daily movement patterns, especially during the "traditional" breeding period. Many hunters, along with quite a few biologists and other scientists, claim that the phase of the lunar cycle changes absolutely nothing when it comes to deer movement and behavior. Others will swear that a full moon makes secretive whitetails more unpredictable than ever. I tend to agree with the latter group.

Up until a few years ago, I maintained a daily journal that detailed every aspect of each and every day I spent in the deer woods for each of 20 seasons. On those pages, I would briefly detail the temperature, wind direction, weather conditions, moon phase and other bits of information, such as hunting pressure, condition of the mast crop, predominate agricultural crops in the area, and when the crops were being harvested. From all of this I learned one very important fact – that the phase of the moon affects whitetail movement as much as any other factor.

In some years the full moon fell during the pre-rut, in some at the height of the rut, and in others not until well into the post-rut. But during each of those years the rut still took place, usually within just a few days of its traditional start – no matter what phase the moon was in.

My most productive years proved to be those when the full moon occurred near the end of the third week in November. Where I live in the Midwest, the rut traditionally begins around November 8th or 9th. When the full moon falls around the 21st or 22nd, the rut kicks in during the dark of a new moon. During those years when the dark of the moon tended to coincide with the rut, I observed an average of 9.8 deer each day during the week prior to the 8th or 9th and during the week following those dates. During those years when there was a full moon at the outset of the rut, the average number of deer observed each day from my stands during the same 2-week period dropped to less than 3. And during this period, I hunt each and every day.

There is nothing scientific about my independent study. These have simply been my personal observations, and some years the findings were influenced by drought, heat, poor mast-crop production, stormy weather, standing corn, etc., etc. But of all factors, the moon phase seems to have had the most dramatic impact in the average number of deer seen each day. In short, during the dark of the moon, whitetails tend to move more during daylight hours. And during a full moon, deer move mostly at night. It's as simple as that – period!

The Best Way to
Harvest a Record-Class Buck

with Jerry Martin

While whitetails are found and hunted across a majority of the United States, most of the lower half of Canada, and southward into South America, there are a few places which have won deserved reputations for producing more than their fair share of trophy-class bucks. And in many of these big-buck hot spots, what is considered just a good average buck could be the buck of a lifetime for deer hunters throughout much of the whitetail's range. With that said, *the first step in taking a record-class buck is hunting in an area that holds record-book bucks.*

Many whitetail hunters in the Southeast hunt their entire lives and never once lay eyes upon a tall-tined, heavy-horned buck that may score 150 Boone and Crockett points. To these hunters a

buck that tops 125 points could be the best buck they ever take, or get the chance to harvest. And here a buck that tops 130 points would indeed be considered a true trophy-class whitetail. However, that same class of buck wouldn't even be considered a "shooter" where trophy hunters have their sights set on taking a buck that tops 150 points. And to get the opportunity to get such a buck in their sights, deer hunters across the country are now doing a lot more traveling to hunt such a big-buck-producing Mecca.

One dedicated whitetail hunter who enjoys the enviable opportunity to spend most of each fall hunting some of the finest trophy-producing areas of North America is Jerry Martin, senior hunting advisor for Bass Pro Shops. In a single season, this

Wooded river valleys often hold the largest bucks in a particular area.

veteran deer hunter often gets more chances at trophy-class whitetails than most of us experience in our lives. He too has favorite places to hunt for the bucks of his dreams.

"Do your homework about the buck-producing capabilities of an area before spending good money to book with an outfitter, or to apply for a permit. All the time spent making phone calls, researching the trophy potential of the area, talking with area hunters and landowners, studying hunter success, determining the best times to hunt a particular area, and other such things are good investments to insure that you get a fair chance at taking the kind of buck you're going after. Never simply put all of your trust into what someone else has told you and head for an area just because a few really big bucks

came from there. If you do, don't be too disappointed if you head home without a nice buck lying in the back of your pickup!" warns Martin.

This successful trophy-buck hunter consistently fills his tag because he does his homework. Jerry realizes that the windows for taking truly magnificent bucks are at best short. His efforts must reward him with not only the quality of buck he has determined to meet his personal standards, but very often a buck that will also allow him to put together the hunting video or television show he's in the area to shoot. You won't find him wasting his time where the potential to take a dandy whitetail is low. The following are his top five picks for taking a trophy-class whitetail buck, possibly one of record-book proportions.

Jerry Martin's Top Five

Kansas

Topping Jerry Martin's list of favorite places to take an impressive whitetail buck is the state of Kansas. A number of regions within the state have regularly produced Boone-and-Crockett-class bucks of almost exaggerated dimensions, but the prairie country of west and west-central Kansas remains Martin's favorite. And for good reason. He's taken several tremendous bucks there, including one true monster typical buck that gross-scored more than 200 Boone and Crockett points!

"This region of the state annually gives up quite a few big bucks. The soil here is extremely high in minerals and the deer have exceptional genetics. However, just as important is the fact that the deer see very little hunting pressure and more of the bucks reach prime age. All of these things are important to producing record-book-class whitetails," Martin points out.

Iowa

The "Hawkeye State" has also earned a reputation for producing some outstanding whitetail bucks. One thing is for certain – in this heavily farmed Midwestern state, the deer never go for want of

quality food sources. Only a small percentage of the state is actually deer habitat, and most of it can be found all along the Mississippi River drainage down the eastern side of the state, all across the southern tier of counties that border Missouri, and up along the western boundary of the state. Fully 75 percent of Iowa sees heavy agriculture, leaving little room for large stands of timber or brush for deer.

However, where there is suitable cover, there are usually deer. Iowa is home to some 250,000 whitetails that inhabit only about a fourth of the state's land mass. And within the good habitat found in many areas the deer density can be reasonably high. Jerry Martin's pick for hunting this state is the south-central region, in those counties that butt up against the Missouri line – Davis, Appanoose, Wayne, Decatur and Ringgold. Good deer numbers, outstanding genetics, plenty of food and an abundance of good bucks promise the visiting hunter ample opportunities.

Iowa bowhunters enjoy hunting the rut all to themselves. Other than an early muzzleloader season in October, all deer hunting in the state until early December is with bow and arrow. And during the two back-to-back short gun seasons, hunters can only use either a shotgun loaded with slugs or a muzzleloading rifle. The limited range of these firearms insures that many good bucks survive the annual harvest of more than 100,000

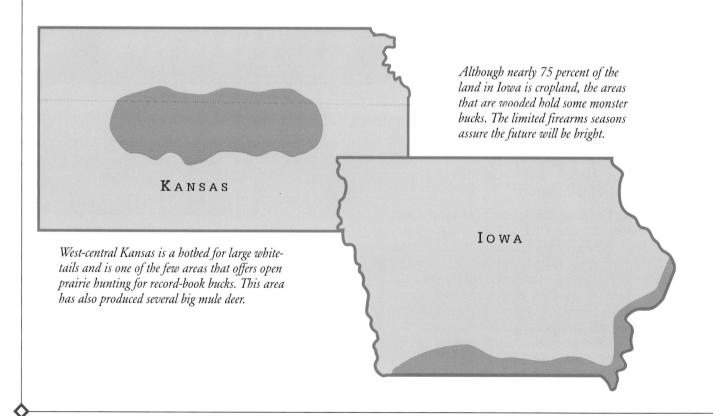

Although nearly 75 percent of the land in Iowa is cropland, the areas that are wooded hold some monster bucks. The limited firearms seasons assure the future will be bright.

West-central Kansas is a hotbed for large whitetails and is one of the few areas that offers open prairie hunting for record-book bucks. This area has also produced several big mule deer.

gun-taken whitetails, the vast majority of which are does. Muzzleloaders do enjoy a final hunt from just before Christmas into early January, but the hunting can be tough – AND COLD.

Illinois

The best-known big-buck-producing region of this state is what is often referred to as "The Golden Triangle" – a four-county area located between the confluence of the Illinois and Mississippi Rivers. The leading buck producer within this region has consistently been Pike County, which also happens to be Illinois' largest county. In recent years, this county alone has annually attracted more than 5,000 nonresident bowhunters. To lighten the hunting pressure, the Illinois Department of Natural Resources is now placing a limit on the number of nonresident permits issued.

Martin feels that the region has simply gotten too much attention, and while the number of good bucks there remains relatively high, so has the competition for hunting them. Finding properties that offer quality buck opportunities has gotten increasingly difficult, and more expensive. His choice for a higher chance at taking a quality Illinois buck would now be one of the counties that border the so-called "Golden Triangle" counties of Calhoun, Pike, Adams and Brown.

He tends to favor Scott County, which lies across the Illinois River to the east of Pike County. Much of the county offers the same topography as the more famous county to its west, including a rich and wide river plain and broken hardwood ridges with a good mix of farmland. Martin feels that the lighter hunting pressure in this county, and in the counties just to the north and south as well, results in better-quality buck-hunting opportunities.

Missouri

With a million or more deer statewide, Missouri offers good deer hunting just about everywhere within its borders. However, Jerry Martin points out that the biggest bucks and the highest deer densities are found across the northern portion of the state. And here he tends to favor certain counties that border Iowa – namely Putnam, Schuyler, Scotland and Clark.

This region is a nearly ideal mix of rolling hardwood-covered ridges, broken tracts of heavily farmed grain fields, CRP lands, hay fields for cattle production and more than a fair share of abandoned farm sites. In recent years it has produced some of the state's best bucks.

"Northern Missouri offers a good break between forest and crop lands, and this belt that runs along the Iowa border for about 40 miles south continually produces high numbers of big bucks," claims Martin.

North-central Missouri tends to produce many large bucks. The mix of prime habitat types offers deer perfect conditions to thrive.

Martin favors the west-central counties in Illinois. However, he tends to avoid the famous Pike County, due to the number of hunters that now descend upon its deer woods each fall.

Nebraska

Like its neighbor to the east (Iowa), this state is home to what may seem to be a relatively low deer population. From north to south, east to west, Nebraska is home to barely 300,000 deer, and only about half of those are of the whitetail variety. Mule deer make up the other half, found primarily in the western half of the state. But here again, deer-holding habitat makes up only about 30 percent of the state. Generally speaking, the remainder of the state is intensely cropped or made up of sparse grasses and dry high plains where deer are either practically nonexistent or extremely low in number. However, find good habitat with food, water and cover, and you'll generally find deer.

One such place is along the Republican River of south-central Nebraska. This is one of Jerry's favorite whitetail hunting hot spots. The area offers plenty of agriculture for a plentiful whitetail food source, a continual water supply and heavy river-bottom cover for the deer. Martin regularly hunts near the town of Arapahoe, on a piece of property where it's not uncommon to see upwards of 200 whitetails a day. While the buck-to-doe ratio in this area is way out of balance, there are still plenty of big bucks to choose from. Finding a farm or ranch to hunt on is the biggest problem the hunter faces here. The limited availability of lands to hunt places a premium on quality habitat. However, several reputable outfitters within the region can offer a hunter an excellent opportunity to take a 150-plus-class buck.

Top areas in Nebraska include river valleys along the southern border of the state. The valleys tend to form travel corridors for big bucks.

NEBRASKA

Every whitetail hunter has a favorite deer camp or hunting spot. Sometimes what makes the location so special is simply the company of the other hunters with whom you share the annual ritual known as deer season. Other places become special because of the huge bucks that leave us with everlasting dreams. And when a hunt or camp successfully combines both, it captures a very special place in our memories and in our hearts.

Nestled along the banks of the meandering Niobrara River of north-central Nebraska, the Arrowsmith ranch has become one of those places for me. The first time I ever laid eyes on the ranch I was riding with Nebraska conservation officer Bruce Weibe, of Bassett. I was looking for a spot to hunt Merriam's wild turkey, and Bruce had kindly offered to take me out and introduce me to ranch owner Brad Arrowsmith. As he drove the 15 miles out to the ranch from town, Bruce praised the quality of deer and turkey hunting in the area. But as we headed out across sandy plains covered with sparse grass, I could count the trees in sight practically on one hand. I couldn't imagine where all of this fantastic hunting took place. Then we broke over the rim of the Niobrara River canyon.

Rising up from the wide, shallow and lazy river were long wooded points covered with everything from oaks to ponderosa pines, with grassy valleys and a patchwork of river-bottom hay fields broken by sizeable stands of timber and wooded fence lines. The country was everything any whitetail could ask for, with plenty of feed plus an abundance of cover. And as I later discovered, it was more than any whitetail hunter could dream of, as I immediately began to realize the moment I walked into the Arrowsmith home and spotted a 190-class buck hanging on the wall.

Likewise, Brad Arrowsmith turned out to be everything one could imagine a Nebraska cattle rancher to be, only this cattle rancher also has a passion for hunting whitetail deer. And in addition to working a sizeable herd of cattle, he also intensively manages his 18,000-acre ranch to produce quality bucks. While he does leave ample alfalfa in his hay fields for the deer, plus some

GREAT DAYS ON THE NIOBRARA

by Toby Bridges

The Niobrara River valley

corn standing to help see the whitetails through a tough winter, he does not go out of the way to plant a large number of food plots. Between the oaks, snowberries, sumac, and tremendous amount of other browse, the deer on the Arrowsmith ranch remain fat and sassy. And due to this rancher's tight limits on the number of mature bucks harvested each season, there are always plenty of 150-plus whitetails to be found. During most seasons at least one buck of Boone and Crockett proportions comes from the ranch, while some of the other six to eight hunters outfitted on the property each season will also catch a glimpse of such a super buck.

I've enjoyed the opportunity to hunt the ranch several times, and took a good mid 160 class muzzleloader trophy buck there on one hunt. However, the season I remember most is one bitterly cold late muzzleloader hunt during which I convinced Brad to join me.

It was the week before Christmas and as I had feared, just as I pulled into Bassett the evening before, the winds had picked up from out of the North. By morning it was spitting snow and the wind chill was in the –40s. Despite the deep-freeze weather, I found my friend the same warm-hearted person I'd come to know 10 years earlier. The weather meant he would have to devote most of his time to chopping out frozen water tanks and hauling to various pastures the 10 or 12 big round bales of hay his cattle consumed each day. But he still found plenty of time to hunt with me.

During the 6-day hunt, I spotted numerous good bucks, and a few truly outstanding book-class

whitetails. One afternoon I even watched as four near-200-point muley bucks eased across a bare knoll nearly 2 miles away – and on the neighbor's ranch. While I could have dropped a half-dozen 140-class whitetails with my muzzleloader, I held out for one of the bigger bucks, especially a beautiful tall-racked 8-pointer I had seen several times in one of the river-bottom hay fields. What made the upper-150-class buck so special is that it displayed both whitetail and mule deer characteristics. The buck was a definite cross.

On the last afternoon of my hunt, the wind-chills had dropped to almost –60 degrees, and staying out was brutal. I bundled up and covered one hay field, while Brad took refuge in one of his haystacks in another alfalfa field. About a half-hour before sunset more than 30 whitetails fed into the field directly in front of me, including a good 10-pointer. With the sun on the way down, I decided to take the shot and cleanly dropped the buck at nearly 150 yards.

As I admired the buck in the last light of the day, a shot rang out from the haystack a half-mile away. When I drove over, there sat one happy rancher with his first muzzleloader buck, the big 8-point hybrid. It was the perfect end to a perfect hunt.

Brad Arrowsmith books a limited number of trophy-buck hunts on his ranch each season. For more information contact him at Dream Hunts, Inc., HC 88, Box 61, Bassett, NE 68714.

Plan Ahead

So, there you have Jerry Martin's five top picks of places to go for hunting quality whitetail bucks. To further insure the success of his efforts, he hunts private lands exclusively. With the current interest in quality deer management by landowners, more emphasis is now being put on harvesting only mature 4½- or 5½-year-old bucks. Where hunting pressure is closely regulated and the number of bucks harvested limited by a strict quota, Martin realizes that the odds of locating, patterning and eventually getting a shot at a trophy whitetail are more in his favor.

A growing number of state game departments are now beginning to practice quality deer management, and this often includes strict quotas on permits available to hunt a specific area or management zone. And where there are such quotas, the number allotted to nonresidents can be quite small. If you are planning to hunt one of these areas or units, you may find that it could take 3 or more years just to draw a permit. In some states, applications for these permits must be submitted as early as January or February for a hunt the next fall or winter, eliminating spur-of-the-moment hunts.

Top Buck-Producing States

The five states Martin spotlighted at the beginning of this chapter are his favorites for consistently producing big trophy whitetail bucks. Many of the other experts featured in this book may favor other hot spots within these states but would tend to agree with him that those states are currently producing the most impressive harvest of record-book-quality bucks.

The following section is a quick look at these and other top buck-producing states, providing statistics regarding the size of the state's whitetail population and the number of resident hunters, information on how to contact the individual game departments for regulations and season dates, plus in some cases a look at the potential for future trophy-buck production.

Colorado

This state is not necessarily known as a big whitetail producer when it comes to overall harvest numbers, but where the whitetail is found in Colorado, the state does offer great opportunities to take a 150- to 160-class buck. Whitetails are found primarily in the very

northeastern corner of the state, and down along the eastern border. Habitat is limited, and the whitetail population here is around 10,000. Hunters annually harvest around 1,000 to 1,500 whitetails. The deer are found almost exclusively on private lands. For more information contact: Colorado Division of Wildlife, 6060 Broadway, Denver, CO 80216.

Idaho

Whitetails in this Rocky Mountain state are found primarily in the northeastern portion of the state. Idaho is home to approximately 38,000 to 40,000 whitetails, and where they are hunted success rates are very high. In this state greater emphasis is put on hunting the more abundant mule deer, and in some parts of the whitetail's range the deer see very light hunting pressure. As a result, some very good 150- to 160-class bucks are taken. For season dates and permit information contact: Idaho Fish & Game Department, 600 South Walnut, P.O. Box 25, Boise, ID 83707.

Illinois

The best whitetail hunting in the "Prairie State" is generally found all along the Mississippi River and in the southern portion of the state. Illinois is now home to an estimated 750,000 whitetails, with the highest deer densities found in the counties of Calhoun, Pike and Brown in the west-central portion of the state, and in Union, Jackson, Williamson, Randolph, Perry, Franklin, Pulaski and Pope counties in the southern tip. In these areas the density can be 40 or more deer per square mile. The number of shotgun/muzzleloader hunters in the state is around 190,000, with an annual deer harvest of just over 100,000 whitetails. For season dates and permit application information contact: Illinois Department of Natural Resources, 524 2nd Street, Springfield, IL 62701.

Iowa

The counties located along the Missouri border from about center of the state eastward to the Mississippi River and those situated in the very northeastern corner of the state have the highest deer densities, with 30 or so deer per square mile. These areas also produce some of Iowa's best bucks, and likewise receive the greatest demand for the limited number of nonresident permits allocated to these management units.

Another portion of the state that offers plenty of deer and lighter hunting pressure is the Loess Hills region stretching up along the western side of the state. In recent years, between 100,000 and 110,000 gun hunters have harvested just over 100,000 whitetails annually. For more information contact: Iowa Department of Natural Resources, Wallace State Office Building, Des Moines, IA 50319.

Kansas

With all the focus on hunting the super bucks found in Kansas, the game department feels that not enough antlerless (doe) deer are being harvested. New management practices will now focus on getting the buck-to-doe ratio in better balance, with the ultimate goal to produce even better-quality trophy bucks in the future. Consistent big-buck producers continue to be the southwest and northwest quadrants of the state. Around 75,000 gun hunters annually harvest around 85,000 deer here. For information about season dates and permit availability contact: Kansas Department of Wildlife & Parks, 512 S.E. 25th Avenue, Pratt, KS 67124.

Minnesota

The big-buck hunting in this state has remained something of a well-guarded secret. More than 1 million deer inhabit the state, with some of the highest deer densities and best hunting opportunities found in the southeastern corner of the state. Some very impressive Boone-and-Crockett-class bucks have come from the high wooded ridges overlooking the Mississippi River. Just a little over 450,000 gun hunters annually harvest around 190,000 deer. For information contact: Minnesota Department of Natural Resources, Division of Fish & Wildlife, 500 Lafayette Road, St. Paul, MN 55155-4007.

Missouri

The "Show Me State" continues to show resident and visiting nonresident hunters some great deer hunting each fall. The herd here has stabilized at about 1 million deer. The highest deer densities are found across most of the central counties from St. Louis westward and in the extreme northeast. In most of these areas there are around 15 to 30 deer per square mile. Best trophy-buck potential will be found in the agricultural regions from the middle of the state northward. In recent years around 400,000 gun

hunters have harvested just over 200,000 whitetails annually. For season dates contact: Missouri Department of Conservation, 2910 West Truman Blvd., Jefferson City, MO 65102.

Montana

Despite a few harsh winters and significant loss of deer to winterkill in the far northeastern portion of the state during recent years, whitetail numbers throughout the remainder of the state are doing well. Some of the best whitetail densities are found along the Missouri River and numerous other rivers and creeks that drain into it in the eastern half of the state, with more than 45 deer per square mile recorded in some of these areas. Another whitetail hotspot is found near Missoula, with similar deer densities. These areas are often credited with being the "best places in America to take a 150-class whitetail buck." For more information contact: Montana Department of Fish, Wildlife & Parks, P.O. Box 200701, Helena, MT 59620-0701.

Nebraska

In this plains state, about 65,000 gun hunters annually harvest close to 35,000 deer. In some of the more popular big-buck areas, nonresidents may find it difficult to obtain modern gun tags, which are allocated on a draw system. However, these same areas can be hunted during the muzzleloader season that runs most of December. This tag is a "statewide" permit and can be purchased right over the counter. For more information on hunting the "Cornhusker State," contact: Nebraska Game & Parks Commission, 2200 N. 33rd, Lincoln, NE 68503.

Ohio

For almost as long as whitetails have been sport-hunted in this country, Ohio has continually produced some tremendous bucks. Today there are around 310,000 gun hunters in the sate, and they annually harvest close to 100,000 whitetails. In recent years the state has produced some high-ranking record-book bucks, including the largest non-typical whitetail buck ever harvested by a bowhunter. Some of the highest deer densities, along with many of the best buck-producing counties, can be found along the east-central part of the state. For more information on season dates and permit information contact: Ohio Division of Wildlife, 1840 Belcher Drive, Columbus, OH 43228.

Texas

This state is home to more than 4 million deer, the vast majority of which are whitetails. Some 550,000 gun hunters annually take more than 400,000 deer. Unfortunate for the "Lone Star State" is the reputation it has gotten for producing sub-standard bucks. Due to the tremendous private quality deer management going on there now, the quality of bucks harvested in Texas continues to improve. On many ranches where it was once rare to take a buck that would score 125 B&C points, hunters are now regularly taking deer in the 150 to 160 class. Areas with the greatest deer densities are those counties found in south-central Texas and those along the coast near Corpus Christi. Some of these areas harbor more than 50 deer per square mile. For more information concerning seasons contact: Texas Parks & Wildlife Department, 4200 Smith School Road, Austin, TX 78744.

Wyoming

This western state is home to a continually growing whitetail population. Along most creek and river drainages the numbers of whitetails are increasing, offering expanded hunting opportunities. However, the largest number of whitetails can be found in the northeastern corner of the state. Several severe winters during the mid-to-late 1990s resulted in a drastic winterkill, but the numbers have recovered quickly and some good bucks are being taken here once again. The bucks harvested by hunters relying on a good outfitter usually will average 150 B&C points, with some 160-class deer taken regularly. Success rates for whitetails often top 60 percent. For more information about season dates and permit applications contact: Wyoming Game & Fish Department, 5400 Bishop Blvd., Cheyenne, WY 82006-0001.

KANSAS JACKPOT

by Jerry Martin

The country of southwest Kansas is extremely open, and while a few isolated pockets of brush here and there may provide cover for the whitetails that live there, the only really decent habitat is found along the few small rivers and creeks that cut through this semi-arid region. I learned of a huge buck along the Cimarron River that had been hunted hard since the opening of the archery season in September and decided to put in some time during the December rifle season to see if I could get him in my sights.

Jerry Martin with a 166⅝-inch Kansas 8-pointer

buck. I quickly assembled a ground blind, then left.

I returned to the spot early in the afternoon and settled in for the rest of the day. Just before dark, deer slowly began filtering through the brush. Then suddenly an excited doe entered the opening near my blind, stopping and looking around every few yards. I knew a buck had to be following or close by and got my rifle ready. Before I knew it a huge buck ran in from the other direction, passing within 7 yards of where I sat. The doe turned and ran directly downwind of my position and immediately winded me. She blew and bolted, and just as the buck began to react, I found him in my scope and fired when the deer was just 18 yards away. The big-bodied trophy whitetail went only a few yards, then went down.

While the big deer had only been seen once during daylight hours since the rut of early November, the sign we found indicated that the deer had been using the heavy river-bottom cover near a 20-acre stand of wheat that had not been combined. It was a good place to begin my hunt and opening morning, December 1st, found me hunting near the edge of the field. And as luck would have it, that brute walked into the open after it had gotten too dark to shoot. The buck was everything I had been told, with huge heavy beams and an impressive spread. Even in the dark, I knew I was looking at a buck that would top 190 Boone and Crockett points.

I returned to the area the next morning, but the wind was all wrong, and I couldn't hunt exactly where I wanted to be, so I spent the morning back in the brush. No buck, so I headed across the river to do some scouting for an afternoon hunt in case the wind continued to blow from the wrong direction. And I found exactly what I what I was looking for – five sizeable cedars within 50 yards of each other that had been heavily rubbed by a mighty big

I'll never forget the sight of that rack when I walked up to the downed deer. The unbelievably heavy rack sported 10 typical points and several small "kicker" points, and had bases bigger around than my wrists. The deer had a gross score of 201, and after deductions the rack still netted 187⅝ points. I knew I had just taken the best buck I would probably harvest in my lifetime.

When Jerry Martin dropped his huge Kansas Boone and Crockett whitetail, he honestly felt that he had taken the best buck he would ever get a chance at tagging. However, the following year he dropped a tremendous Iowa buck with a .50-caliber in-line muzzleloading rifle during the first general gun season. The date was December 2nd, exactly one year after he took his Kansas monster. You can bet this trophy-buck hunter will be hunting somewhere in big whitetail country every year on December 2nd from now on! —Toby Bridges

Index

Contributing Photographers

Charles J. Alsheimer
Bath, NY
© *Charles J. Alsheimer: p. 100*

Toby Bridges
Cape Girardeau, MO
© *Toby Bridges: pp. 2, 28, 35, 66B, 70, 87, 112, 119*

Denver Bryan
www.DenverBryan.com
© *Denver Bryan: p. 97*

Gary Clancy
Byron, MN
© *Gary Clancy: pp. 83BR, 91, 92-93 all*

Michael H. Francis
Bozeman, MT
© *Michael H. Francis: p. 68*

The Green Agency
www.thegreenagency.com
© *Bill Buckley: pp. 8, 72*
© *Bill Vaznis: p. 14*

Donald M. Jones
Troy, MT
© *Donald M. Jones: pp. 44, 56, 78, 83TL, 83TR*

Mark Kayser
Pierre, SD
© *Mark Kayser: back cover TR, back cover BR, pp. 6-7, 42-43, 51*

Bill Kinney
www.BillKinney.com
© *Bill Kinney: back cover TL, p. 107*

Lance Krueger
www.LanceKrueger.com
© *Lance Krueger: pp. 36, 113*

Lon Lauber
www.LonLauber.com
© *Lon Lauber: pp. 4, 66T, 105*

Bill Lea
Franklin, NC
© *Bill Lea: p. 76*

Stephen W. Maas
Wyoming, MN
© *Stephen W. Maas: pp. 18, 71, 81, 82, 111 both*

Bill Marchel
BillMarchel.com
© *Bill Marchel: p. 63*

Mark Raycroft
Trenton, Ontario, Canada
© *Mark Raycroft: pp. 88, 108*

Dusan Smetana
www.DusanSmetana.com
© *Dusan Smetana: pp. 94, 114-115*

Windigo Images
www.windigoimages.com
© *Mike Barlow: p. 57*

(Note: T=Top, C=Center, B=Bottom, L=Left, R=Right, I=Inset)